2

THIS BOOK SHOULD BE RETURNED ON OR BEFORE THE LATEST
DATE SHOWN TO THE LIBRARY FROM WHICH IT WAS BORROWED

AUTHOR

CRIGHTON, D.

CLASS

TITLE

D0993856

L2

DIANA CRIGHTON'S

English Excursions

ESSAYS
ON
ART
ARCHITECTURE
HISTORY
& FOOD

CUMBRIA

LANCASHIRE

NORTHUMBRIA

YORKSHIRE

Northern Journey

EXCURSION | Publishing

Diana Crighton

Northern Journey is the second volume of Diana Crighton's English Excursions following the first on London and the home counties published in 1996. Diana has also written Visiting With Taste, towards a cultural change in design and food for museums and galleries. After an early career in the clothes business, she then trained and worked as a cook and has managed both her own and museum restaurants. She has a degree in History of Art, Architecture and Design; she lectures publicly and to graduates and is now planning the next volume on the South West and subsequently the whole of Great Britain.

She formed a consultancy almost ten years ago which specialises in advising museums and famous locations on the development of the public areas. She has built a reputation for developing their identity. Among her commissions are the cafés at the River and Rowing Museum at Henley-on-Thames, the Millennium Centre at Slimbridge, Gloucestershire, the Geffrye Museum in London, the Swindon Railway Heritage Museum, Nottingham Castle and Birmingham Museum and Art Gallery. She lives in Wells, Somerset.

07845977

Art Direction Diana Crighton
Illustrations Kate Parkin
Cover Design Global Image
Layout Mitou van der Harst-Tricoit
Editing Joanna Roughton
Printing in Padstow by TJ INTERNATIONAL Ltd

Other titles by Diana Crighton
Visiting With Taste
English Excursions Home Counties and London

Excursion Publishing
24 New Square South Horrington Wells Somerset BA5 3JS

ISBN 0-9528334-1-7

Addresses

4

Prologue

The picture on the front cover of this book which I took in Swaledale on a midsummer's eve epitomises this Northern journey: a voyage of contrasts, splendour and simplicity, images of clarity with an intricate history. As I stood and gazed at a minster or ruined abbey, or at these ancient fields and barns, the impact was equally amazing and arresting.

As I criss-crossed the counties I came upon views which were unbearably beautiful, which J M W Turner had painted more than 200 years ago. There were more which live up to the picture Samuel Taylor Coleridge described, of the Lakes from his study window at Greta Bridge 'as if heaven & earth were forever talking to each other'. I visited inspirational buildings, rediscovered elegant architecture, tasted some exceptional regional food and was enchanted by Northerners. This is my way of travelling – holistically.

I rummage around for traditions and repeatedly enquire: 'Is it local?' Locally grown and prepared, is the food which best complements this kind of sauntering, or 'allacking' as one does in Yorkshire, which has the lion's share of this book because it is quite simply the largest in the region. What tempts me to loiter and return is agreeable company, home baking, excellent tea, bread with a provenance, cheese with a pedigree and the taste of the moment. My explorations paid off. I uncovered these characteristics in unexpected destinations, high up on a windswept fell or in a bustling parish church vestry tea room. The best cooking in the North is layered with good produce, such as leeks one might write an ode to, the subtle nuances of Lancashire cheese, creamy and eminently cookable, or Wensleydale, crumblier, paler with no less of a personality. Their respective attributes have the makings of a taste debate, but not another War of the Roses.

I seem destined to be a traveller, I first discovered this region more than thirty years ago wearing a different hat; hats were virtually uniform if you were in the clothes business when some dress shops were still selling gowns. In the course of launching a very young collection on the unsuspecting country I had to scour towns and cities looking for the best shops and stores. There were no dresses to carry, but I did carry the memories and images of the northern counties with me for a long time, memories of towns, still manufacturing and still smoking, where the contrast of moor or dale was sharper as it rose up at the end of a street. Over the last two years my course led me to destinations where the car has not quite taken over, where the street markets are still thriving and the small shops like those in Appleby and Cockermouth still knit the community together.

Last but not least, the ingredient which gives me the greatest pleasure in this travel pudding is the people with whom I share a table, talk to, and stay. I now have a long list of new friends in museums, libraries, information centres and on farms. I would like to thank everyone I met for their hospitality, help and time.

CUMBRIA

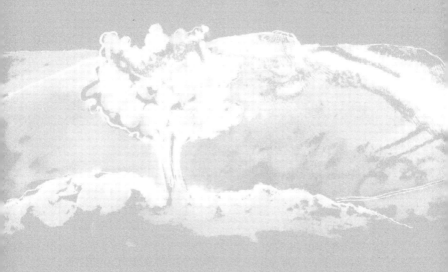

1

Abbot Hall Art Gallery and the Museum of Lakeland Life and Industry

Kendal, Cumbria

A few steps away from the epicentre of the market town of Kendal I found Abbot Hall, an elegant town house thought to have been designed in limestone by that so prolific of Yorkshire architects John Carr, a hero of this book. For he turned the Georgian house into an art form, just as Lady Anne Clifford is a heroine for her crusade of restoring her medieval and Norman castles in Cumbria and Yorkshire.

Abbot Hall Art Gallery and the Museum of Lakeland Life opposite built in 1762, are bordered by the River Kent and surrounded by pleasure grounds constructed about a hundred years ago. Yet another classical building of 1823, the Gas Meter House by Francis Webster has been preserved and rebuilt here, which with the church and river promenade forms a very handsome group.

Viewing the gallery and museum before looking at the town was an ideal introduction to the social and industrial life responsible for so many of the other elegant public buildings. It also fixes the start of the Picturesque movement which put the Lakes on the map, encouraging artists and poets to depict that 'other place' perspective to which so many have been drawn. Abbot Hall itself was rented out to those questing for the picturesque in the late eighteenth century, the style seekers of their day. But the Museum of Lakeland Life also gives hints of the Arts and Crafts movement, the spinners, weavers and furniture makers. Kendal must have been a visually interesting place at the turn of the twentieth century.

You reach the gallery through an archway after ascending an exterior symmetrical staircase. In a state of disrepair, it was restored by the local civic society in the 1950s and opened as a museum in the early 1960s. The paintings by George Romney, bought by the founder of the gallery, are the base of an engaging collection, of which a considerable amount is related to the Lake District.

The entrance hall with its classical columns sets the formal scene which follows, where many pictures and contemporary pieces of furniture are shown in an unfettered environment. There are no ropes. The place is calm and uncluttered with slate floors and bay windows giving views over to the river; ornate plasterwork, pretty shutters and furniture take the eye. The north western reputation for elegant furniture is interpreted where setting complements pieces such as the Gillow secretaires, made in Lancaster. A beautiful Sheraton card table is placed among the serene Romney portraits, the most enchanting of Lady Hamilton who came from the area, in pen and wash, are interspersed with cabinets housing Delft and a piece of Leeds creamware, a tea pot with a nautical decoration.

All the ground-floor rooms have absorbing plasterwork (Romney did not like exuberant mouldings, he preferred a less florid design), yet there are painted rooms and some have wallpaper. The dining room is painted in a soft green, considered to be the colour that aided digestion. Why do so many paint them red? Here the panelling has a classical early eighteenth-century treatment and is not picked out or embellished, a room which conveys the idea of classical orders. The cornice should be read as the capital, the wall as the columns, and the area below the dado as the base or pediment. To the purists, the guide tells us, any decoration would be a distraction from the orders. On the other hand the room, with its House of Lords Pugin-like wallpaper and three-dimensional carved dado, makes a flamboyant contrast.

In addition to the Romney pictures the gallery has a reputable collection of eighteenth-century portraits reflecting the rise of the landed gentry and aristocracy often set in their own parkland; a particularly poignant portrait of a child by Christopher Steel shows a young boy with a pigeon in front of Cartmel Priory. The collection is, however, well rounded. There is contemporary work of a completely different style and contrast of the twentieth-century interwar years, one of which I am particularly fond is Ben Nicholson's still life, Crowned Head, quite magnificent in a rich terracotta colour. Among other twentieth-century artists whose work was influenced by the area is Peter Lanyon, and there is a collage by Kurt Schwitters, as well as work by Percy Kelly (see page 16). And there are connections with the St Ives school through Ben Nicholson, his sister Winifred and of course Barbara Hepworth. The connection I sought was an earlier one, the portrait of Lady Anne Clifford by Sir John Bracken, of which she was most fond; there is a copy of the large triptych with Lady Anne portrayed as a young woman, middle-aged with her Lady of Shallot hair and in old age, which hangs at Appleby Castle but belongs to Abbot Hall. This is a charming gallery and helps you to get into the landscape which each artist pictured in their period. Rarely is one able to stroll around such an elegant house and be permitted to gaze and study the work so freely.

Across the courtyard is the Museum of Lakeland Life which has a series of room settings and a Victorian Kendal Street scene with shops. The chemist has all the proper drawers and cut-glass knobs, the whole interior coming from Ulverston twenty miles away. There are representations of a brewery, a photographer, Mr Stubbs the tailor and cutter with his garment presses and, of course, the shoe industry which developed from tanning and hide curing. A large case of shoes has some high buttoned boots, and a delightful collection of children's shoes acquired by K's, the shoemakers, penny stalls and a haberdasher. All the raw materials that helped Lakeland life are here: the signs and signifiers of the industries, where everything that was available had to be used and natural resources were developed into industries.

Minerals were mined, graphite came from Borrowdale for pencils, wood was turned for pipes and bobbins, larger for spinning and weaving and smaller for the Silko reels. Hazel, willow and oak coppicing produced long lengths of wood left to season for a year and then carved into various sizes for each purpose. Every artefact tells a story of nineteenth-century industry and farming life: wood, iron ore, lead, zinc, gypsum, lime, tungsten, silver and, of course, the staple wool. Not least there is a large loom, the last original to survive in Kendal. And something that I remembered from childhood, a brushing machine made with the teazles that you see growing by the wayside. Perhaps the most extraordinary piece of folk art is a miner's carving of a grotto, the mining equivalent of the ship in a bottle and the real art of industry. What has happened to the skills of those who managed to create such intricate pieces of work from minerals and crystals?

The costume exhibits show that eighteenth-century Lakeland ladies had slender waists. And as for textiles, there has always been a tradition of weaving. At the turn of the last century, possibly influenced by John Ruskin, two ladies, Anne and Francis Garnett, set up the Spinneries at Bowness and managed it for nearly 40 years. Their production included some of the most beautiful fabrics made in England: light silk throws, linens and materials with metal thread, where the textures were inspired by the environment, the lakes, the fells and stones and gardens. And Lakeland furniture was made by Arthur Simpson of Kendal (closed as recently as 1951) in the Arts and Crafts idiom for Voysey's house at Littlehome at nearby Windermere. Among the beautiful pieces of local furniture are a delicate handled sideboard and the kind of court cupboards I was to see at Townend (see page 25). There are few examples of vernacular housing before the seventeenth century as the earliest farmhouses were temporary, constructed of wood with rubble infill of wattle and bracken, because of the constant danger of Scottish invasions. With unsettled conditions in the borders there was little incentive to build permanent housing except for the large fortified farms and pele towers. There is one at Dalemain. So between the seventeenth and nineteenth centuries farmers reinterpreted earlier models in stone when their houses became more permanent. This rich collection mirrors the busy town, and helps to piece together the architecture of the courts and buildings.

Lakeland cooking once took place on so-called back stones where good pastry, hasty puddings and stewed venison were prepared. The kitchens were all panelled, again like Townend. Here in a reinstated example the apples are drying on a rack for the winter, there is a comforting, warm feeling and a cat stares mesmerised at the fire where a watercolour of the Eden Valley hangs. The vernacular furniture, the sumptuously carved court cupboard and the panelling are in their way are just as pleasing as the designer-made Sheraton across the courtyard. But the food and robust fuelling country dishes are not on the menu. Nevertheless the gallery coffee shop does you very well and is relaxing after all this looking. It forms a good sandwich between the two museums, yet without the colour of oak which proliferates in the museum. They may not be able to prepare more than one or two hot dishes but the modest choices are nicely served by exceptionally pleasant and friendly staff. One such dish might be home-produced pâté with a Cumberland sauce, both regional like the local sausages, cheese and soup. Lakeland ice cream is offered and although the Borrowdale baking has not arrived here in force there are homemade sponges and tray bakes aplenty. Contemporary exhibitions adorn the wall, and there is a real sense of being included in the atmosphere of Abbot Hall.

In many old Lakeland recipes sharp fruit and spices predominate: one finds that baking flavourings were rum and ginger. I would like to find something more of the damson in its season in the baking. And of course high teas in this district were once very substantial, with pies and puddings and no doubt potted char, described by William Camden as a sort of 'golden Alpine Trout' (it lives in the cold deep water from Windermere), and home-cured mutton and beef. Lady Anne Clifford noted in her day books, which are kept in the county record office, the dates she ordered sugar loaves from Penrith and how much she paid her

staff to preserve fruit for the winter. Such fruity flavours contrast well in winter with spices; again Lady Anne recorded the purchase of nutmeg from a Mr Edmund Middleton in 1673 along with 'raysons', currants and capers, bought in perhaps from the ports on the east coast. Given the opportunity and time Abbot Hall, I felt, would harvest these ideas, absorb and refine the traditions in its own inimitable style.

2

Appleby-in-Westmorland

Cumbria

Appleby, the former county town of Westmorland, is in the Eden Valley and grew from a large loop of the River Eden, with the two sections being divided by a bridge. As Camden wrote in 1610, it is 'environed almost wholly with the river'. Appleby is renowned for its horse fair, when the whole horse world and travellers meet here in June.

The town was sacked by the Scots and I wondered if the street called Doomgate or even Scattergate was a legacy from this episode. The many-hued pink and red stone which gives this town, other villages and settlements in the Eden Valley their character dates from the Permo-Triassic age; the colours vary from pale shrimp pink to deep red at Brampton, with many gradations in between and some sparkle. This red geological thread runs from the west coast of Cumbria to the edge of the lakes and into the green valley between them and the Pennines.

Boroughgate is the main street with some fine buildings. It climbs up to the castle and, like Warkworth, has the church at the lower end. Appleby has to be visited as part of Lady Anne Clifford's trail for she spent much of her latter years living at her castle and was buried here. I wanted to see her resting place and the buildings which she diligently restored. Lady Anne was a true Renaissance woman, restorer and fighter, and must have appreciated architecture and design. She may well have absorbed the latest styles at the Carolean court as a lady in waiting where she met Inigo Jones who designed a mask dress for her in 1609. She was an innovator in her own right, and through connections by birth and two marriages was related to the top echelons of the aristocracy. At Appleby she restored two buildings: the parish church of St Lawrence and Appleby Castle and built an orderly group of almshouses. She also put up her mother's memorial in this church.

The entrance to St Lawrence is deceptive; it dates from 1200 although the church itself was built in 1300. The tower, also like Warkworth, was a refuge from marauders and the large nave was built for prayer, assemblages and meetings where important books were kept: Fox's Acts and Monument of the Martyrs, first published in 1563, is still chained here. The memorial carvings are sumptuous and the exceptional organ came from Carlisle Cathedral. The pews are carved with strips of open fretwork, some upholstered in thick blanket-like material, doubtless ensuring that the most important members of the congregation did not suffer from the cold in the pews in front of the pulpit. A touch of the nineteenth century and early Gothic links the church with the market square where in 1811 Robert Smirke, who designed the British Museum, conceived an elegant screen to replace the cloisters, where butter was sold; today it is rather defiled by insensitive advertising. At the time of its design, local dignitaries said it would have cost half as much if it had been done by a local.

There is one house on Boroughgate which has been designed and decorated with extraordinary bravura; the White House with its profusion of pale green ogee arches above every window. Built in 1756, it appears to precede the Picturesque revival by at least twenty years. It was built by Jack Robinson, the notorious MP whose slogan was 'Quick as a flash'. Almost opposite is one of the earliest buildings, the Moot Hall, where the carved plaque of 1179 denotes the date of the first known charter, and houses the tourist information office and council chamber. On the right is a house with a charming possibly early nineteenth-century hand painted sign of a tobacco seller, fading, yet still elegant under a shell portico. There is a bevy of food stalls, with fish and flowers clustered around the Moot Hall which add a degree of activity, and Appleby has some interesting street names. I discovered that wiend, as in Shaw's Wiend, means way.

Appleby has two crosses: High at the top of Boroughgate which was once the site of a cheese market and Low at the other end. Half way up on the left, through an entrance opening up to quadrangle one finds Lady Anne's almshouses which appear as neat as the day they were built. The windows are painted in deep crimson against the pink stone with stone carvings in the corners. I sensed her spirit more strongly here than at the castle. The quality of the housekeeping would make her proud of her legacy.

If there is one elegant food shop here it is Ewbanks the butcher near the Moot Hall, which places its produce on display as though it were precious; not for them the higgledy-piggledy mass of cuts and platefuls of mince. Ewbanks treats a sirloin as it name warrants, in a royal fashion, taking centre stage almost as an artwork without a hint of Damien Hurst. A large mahogany counter, a relic from an earlier business (possibly haberdashery), has been left. The Ewbanks keep their own cattle and deserve an award for service and dedication.

In matters of provisioning it appears from Lady Anne's day books that she was very much a supporter of local producers. Her wine was sent from Barnard Castle to Brough Castle, further south; twelve gallons and three quarts were bought for one Christmas. Artichokes were grown at Brougham, where the garden was well watered by the Easmont. In June 1674 she had crawfish costing 2/6d from Nappa Hall (nearer to Barden and Skipton) while fruit and spices were also bought for Christmas, dried fruits, raisins, prunes, sugar, nutmegs, cinnamon, pepper and others for £2.13.2. I visualise these ingredients being stirred and made either into one enormous pudding or pie or perhaps finishing as sugared sweetmeats on pewter plates set upon a large oak trestle. Venison was bought from other estates and in 1673 she paid £2.10.0 for ten bushels of malt for brewing beer at Appleby. Her servants Arthur Swinden and Mrs Pate were paid to preserve currants, and were preserving rhubarb as early as December.

Reading through her day books was enthralling, they are a perfect record which tells us what was grown, how much was paid, and to whom. As I sat absorbed with this archive in the county record office at Kendal I felt uncannily close to her times and her life.

Castlegate House Gallery, Cockermouth and Loweswater

Cumbria

There is a good crop of museums and galleries for enthusiasts visiting Cockermouth. Next to Wordsworth House one finds a minute mineral and fossil gallery with illuminated displays and all for a mere 50p, almost a little gem in itself; there is the toy museum, vintage car museum and the Castlegate House Gallery. This last is an elegant double-fronted house, formerly a dower house for and opposite the castle. One finds Adam ceilings and cornices and an exciting mixture of contemporary ceramics and paintings. Stylishly hung selling exhibitions take place through-out the year. I could easily be inveigled into making a winter expedition to Cockermouth.

True to Cockermouth custom Castlegate House is painted, in pink. It was probably built in 1739, and has two elegant reception rooms filled with paintings, both looking out over to the castle. A particularly informal, relaxed yet civilised air pervades as you walk around the rooms where pictures are hung.

Percy Kelly is one of the artists whose paintings are well rep-resented. I had not seen any of his work before, although I have been engrossed with his contemporaries. Kelly was a West Cumbrian, and was adept at both the domestic and natural scene: houses, townscapes churches as well as landscapes in this varied slice of England. Kelly was a graphic artist and a letter maker. He worked more vigorously in charcoal, the medium he used to portray field systems and landscape. His was an encom-passing and inspiring eye and he was accomplished in several media. His watercolours of Brittany remind one of the St Ives school and the work of Christopher Wood (Kelly painted in Cornwall in the 1970s). He also collaborated with Sir Nicholas Sekers, whose company at Whitehaven produced wonderful fab-rics in the 60s; I recall the silks, tweeds and mohair much used by couture fashion houses of the time.

After seeing the rooms visitors can visit and enjoy a hidden walled garden where sculpture is sometimes exhibited in the summer. This is a more contemplative space or open air gallery, crowded with rose-covered arches and parterre, where the sculpture appears to grow from the planting. Ordered lupins rise straight and irises shoot up under apple trees. A ceramic cat sits in a micro-vegetable garden behind the rosemary waiting to pounce on an unsuspecting field mouse. This is not a garden for sitting about, rather to pause among the plants which have been selected for their form and provision of shade. The rear is covered in pink, not paint but flowers: roses, japonica and sweet peas.

My day had begun at Loweswater, and it was good to see Kelly's delicate line drawings of the Lake. Driving from Lorton around these valleys is the best of both worlds. The lanes which had inspired Kelly were full of wild flowers. Dog roses, buttercups, fox gloves, elderflower and ferns grew up from the hedges in a shimmering heat above the water.

Every house along the way had its name carved in white, incised upon grey slate, very cool, right and located. I had stayed the night before at High Stanger Farm, a real, and I mean real, working farm. Alison Hewitson, her husband and son talked with me until the small hours in their small kitchen, of supermarkets, farming and where would it all go. But there was a singular vein of hope with her eighteen-year-old son, who works very hard on the farm with his father. He needed no excuse to talk about his beloved sheep. Sheep were in his soul. He was absolutely engrossed with the land. Farming will survive with this passion. I had not realised that shearing is related to when the lambs are born as the wool rises up on the ewes after weaning. This explained why they were shorn in some areas and still woolly in others. Before shearing, wool used to be gathered and picked up as sheep naturally dropped it.

After Cockermouth I took the top road to Keswick and, as I passed coachloads of today's admirers of the Picturesque, I realised that everyone must have the opportunity to see the beauty of this landscape whether they can walk like Dorothy Wordsworth or not. In this combination of two small counties, as it was sixty years ago, there are examples of almost every kind of topography and geography that England possesses: mountains, valleys, lakes, farmsteads, sheep walks, forests, small county towns and villages.

Dalemain and Aira Force

Cumbria

How fascinating it is to read of writers' different reactions, across the centuries, to the Lake District. One man's terror can be another's wonder, depending on timing and fashion. In the early nineteenth century Charles Lamb wrote that he had been a tourist, walked and visited all the right places, and experienced the 'Romantic'.

Yet Ralph Thoresby who travelled here in the 1670s (contemporary with the alterations to Dalemain), had a 'horror on eyes and ears from the rugged rocks' and the waterfalls that inspired others. He found the fells 'terrifying: Hardnott was 'mighty dangerous'; Fell Foot was better called 'Hell foot' (it probably was on horseback) and the riverets more 'Hell becks'. Daniel Defoe described the hills as 'formidable'. But Lamb took the post chaise from nearby Penrith and found when he arrived in the evening 'the colours so transmuted by the sunshine that we thought we had got into fairyland'.

The Lake district – I prefer Lake counties – is at times on high summer evenings, even when it has been raining, a fairyland giving all travellers a sense of wonder. These wonders are the result of several geological factors. The number of topographical variations in a area which is smaller than Yorkshire is the result of more than 10,000 years of human occupation, modified by settlers and farmers and of course the visitors over the last 250 years.

Today, driving from either Troutbeck or Ambleside, the road to Dalemain is a heavenly looping drive that adjoins Ullswater, the second longest lake which put me right in touch with its activities, and set me in the mood for the house, whose name means valley mansion. It is fortunateley situated with a view of the valley and like so many other Georgian houses this was the last style to be incorporated into an eight bay classical mansion built in a paler shade of the regional sandstone.

It is an atmospheric building and was formerly a twelfth-century pele tower, a fort, with medieval and Elizabethan additions. As you walk through passages and up and down the oak stairs there are clues such as the internal courtyard which reveal its earlier history.

The polished panelled hall shows off the region's art of oak carving, which the warm rose coloured walls complement. The flagstone floor, the elegant flying or cantilevered staircase, a continuous handrail, an unusual oak decorated dado running square to the ceiling and the balusters with a delicate tassel also carved just below the handrail, are all notable. Vases of roses perfume the rooms and the yellow dining room looks over fields, burnished with buttercups, and as it is west facing it also catches the full afternoon sun which sparkles on to the table laid with eighteenth-century Cork glass.

In a small flagstone lobby, the base of the original tower, you will find the small Yeomanry Museum; among the charming collection there is a smart military frock coat with stylish braiding, an aroma of wood smoke pervades the room which has a prize specimen of local furniture, a Cumberland courting chair. These are straight spindle-backed and wide enough to take two. On the first floor of the tower, the Elizabethan part of the house, the atmosphere changes with lower ceilings and plaster fretwork, lower doors and enclosed panelling. It contrasts with the Georgian reception rooms where, continuing my Lady Anne Clifford investigation, I found another portrait of her by Bracken, and there is also a portrait of her father, George Clifford, Earl of Cumberland.

Sir Edward Hasell, who acquired the house in 1679 and altered it in the 1680s, became Lady Anne's secretary on the recommendation of his uncle, the Bishop of Carlisle. Her bequest after her death in 1676 helped him to purchase Dalemain and 'modernise' the house. And Lady Anne made him several gifts for his loyalty and service; one such is the portrait of the 10th Earl of Northumberland, her cousin, a copy of the original Van Dyck which hangs at Alnwick. A portrait of Sir Edward himself by Lely hangs above the carved chimneypiece with swags of acanthus and oak in the drawing room. There is also a reminder that in the years after the Reformation the house sheltered priests who said secret masses and hid here to avoid discovery. Richly carved Jacobean chairs, with their vigorous barley twist outer spindles and cane seats, and panelled oak room, or so called fret-work room, contrast with the palely painted print room and the toy-filled nursery. I like the immediacy of the work or house-keeper's 1920s room, in different manner, with evocative printed lino in that splendid sludgy green, so right for lino – a vacuum cleaner, a hat on a stand, and the ephemera of household needle-work. In the guide book Mrs McCosh writes of the house's ups and downs, the quality which pleases, as well as finding a new dis-covery around each corner. Everywhere one is aware of the fam-ily who have lived and contributed and still live here. As well as portraits on landing walls a montage of black and white family photographs records all manner of occasions and special days. For lovers of Georgian glass there are some air twist examples, in cabinets on the first floor, as well as clothes, and ceramics to please many tastes.

Visitors are also in for a treat when they reach the tea room in the Old Hall, the lord of the manor's dining hall. This is the source of the wood smoke from a large stone fireplace and where an exceedingly long refectory table of about 1670, and around which it seems the room must have been built, is for visitors' enjoyment. Delightful chintz covered chairs bolster the sense of family one gains at Dalemain.

The food is home-based, especially the jams, chutney and jel-lies: grape marmalade, or mixtures of gooseberry with elder-flower, are a ideal combination as is the rhubarb and ginger jam. The home made jellies range from plum and port, Cumberland jelly, redcurrant, and apple mint. All are laid out for you to take for yourself and spread on the scones and tea breads. Local ingre-dients consist of Cumberland sausages made to a local Penrith recipe and Cumberland ham. Hot dishes are robust; the climate can change. Yorkshire puddings are served with a variety of fill-ings; sausage, onions and gravy. Homemade soup could be apple, celery and tomato and Dalemain serves its own version of sticky toffee pudding which seems to be a contemporary Cumbrian spe-ciality. I noted that in 1694 Thoresby, who was so terrified of the terrain was pleased enough to find Jannock bread, oat cake and clap cakes, at Calder Bridge, none of which I have tracked down so far.

The enchanting gardens have a comparable mixture of mood and style to the house – up and down, formal and less formal, spacious or intimate. A wide border planted with the huge-leafed Cranbe, roses, pinks and delicate pink geraniums contrasts with the boxed border garden, lavender, a potting shed and a more formal garden. There is also a rose garden, the source of the perfume and a terrace. Beyond, towards Dacre Beck, a less cultivated area of woodland is planted with rhododendrons. The scale is appealing and the novel way in the children's garden of identifying plants, with pictures or silhouettes of animals will attract small visitors. Secret shady seats are placed for lingering, with a rose arbour and honeysuckle; some walls support plums whilst forget-me-knots, sweet peas, wisteria and ceanothus provide all the shades of pink, blue and lilac you could dream of. The surprises continues; in an alcove I found a delightful eighteenth-century garden seat with twelve separate Hepplewhite backs made in wood, around three sides, with a planked carved seat, and all amusingly, as one long bench.

On another visit to Dalemain from Cockermouth I took, as instructed by a local lady, quite rightly, the 'scenic route'. From Troutbeck as you head to Aira Force, through good pleasant farmland, you travel upwards into the fells through Penruddock. This is pastoral not rugged country, through which, as I told myself, I should not be driving but walking and I did at Aira Force, climbing up the ravine off the sunny road, through contrasting cool glades of birch, ash and oak, up a steep climb of wooden steps to the top. Two young friendly foresters helped me identify the wild flowers; I found lesser stitchwort and much herb Robert in June. Down in the valley of Aira Force you can gather your breath or munch a piece of cake at the wooden tea house, ready for the next stage or excursion to Penrith with its small museum at the seventeenth-century Robinson's School and the Eden Valley beyond.

5

Grasmere, Ambleside, Bridge House and Townend

Cumbria

I was met with an all-enveloping and powerful aroma one damp October evening when I first arrived at Grasmere. This wafted out from an exquisite bothy shop, with a charming sign in sharp green depicting Mrs Nelson, the inventor of the Grasmere biscuit or gingerbread. The next day I found row upon row of biscuits carefully wrapped in greaseproof paper and stacked on shelves. There may only be room for one person at the counter, but this is no museum piece. It is working, or rather baking, and the gingerbread is despatched around the country. This sustaining gingerbread from one of the last such shops in England was more enjoyable than any I have munched; crunchy not dry, properly packed, there is a depth to bite into and, of course, unwrapping the greaseproof was part of the experience.

Any Wordsworth journey should include nearby Rydal House and Dove Cottage in Grasmere, but I was equally interested in finding the places and walks that his sister Dorothy made, for her descriptions of these and the daily round of her and her brother's lives are painted quite eloquently yet succinctly in her journals, with her observations of the seasons, weather and fells. Her energy was admirable. An eighteen-mile walk did not daunt her and her numerous moonlight treks seem almost outlandish to us 200 years later. The diary is useful social history for we find that at the Ambleside fair she noted that many cakes and much beer were sold. She also records a meeting in early October with a lady pedlar from Cockermouth who had been carrying thread and mustard, and seemed well on it, having walked the hills for thirty years.

Dorothy Wordsworth's hills are still 'wrapped in sunshine', rich with orange fern in the autumn. The oaks are dark green and the sycamore was just as she wrote: 'crimson-tufted, the mountain ash a deep orange [with] ashes in their peculiar green'. Dorothy herself was never idle, walking to keep warm, once 'so cold that she ran to the foot of White Moss to get the last bit of warmth'; and she collected mosses to stop the fire. In early

February 1802, she wrote of rain that was too icy to melt the snow, and to keep warm they gathered straw to put around William's shoes while he worked. Once she walked as far as Keswick from Grasmere in the rain. Keswick today struck me as being a town founded on sugar, sugar for energy or shoes; there were many shoeshops, for walking off the excesses. Sweet-toothed Keswick, where its shops are bowed with their burden of chocolates, fudge, meringues, parkin and fruit cake.

As well as copying out William's work, and 'stitching it up', Dorothy kept house, reading to him, endlessly encouraging, and she appeared to enjoy growing vegetables. She noted the sowing, growing, harvesting and eating of peas which connects me with her growing seasons. She picked apples, bottled them in rum, sowed or 'stuck' an inordinate amount of peas as well as beans and broccoli. In a heightened mood on the return to Grasmere after William's wedding she describes three species of flowers in bloom: geraniums, foxglove and buttercups in the water; and on December 21 she noted a large bunch of strawberry blossom. Her walking ethic lived on with Beatrix Potter. I heard from the daughter of one of the writer and conservationist's tenant farmers that she walked from her cottage at Hill Top up to Langdale Pikes in boots and cloak until in her seventies to collect the rent.

I saw, on a wet summer evening when the sun returned, the Furness clog dancers who with their colourful clogs clapped on the slate as they performed their intricate steps outside a pub not far from here.

I am not equipped to follow in Dorothy's footsteps, with energy or words, but the sight of Helm Crag is evidence enough of the Wordsworths' and their friend Coleridge's inspiration from the ever-changing beauty and view from Dove Cottage. These descriptions are best left to one of the original proponents of Lakeland tourism, William Wordsworth himself. Many have followed his ideas. Thomas West compiled a guide to the Lakes in 1807 and Mrs Radcliffe, author of The Mysteries of Udolpho, parodied by Jane Austen in Northanger Abbey climbed this in 1794. She thought Skiddaw, which she and her friends went up on horseback with a guide, a 'tremendous mountain' and they were gripped by 'involuntary horror' and frightened to look into the chasms below. I am not ashamed to write that, even today, taking some of the passes with the protection of a steel box on wheels and five gears, not a horse, still holds an element of danger as the climate can change within half an hour.

In 1694, a century earlier, Ralph Thoresby called nearby Ambleside a 'country vill but of old, as appears by the many heaps of rubbish and ruins of walls as well as paved highways leading thereto, a noted Roman station – Amboglana, as Camden conjectures'. Today old and new join at the river bend by the Bridge House and Adrian Sankey's glasshouse. This workshop also sells pieces while next door the café in a mill is restored with sensitivity.

Bridge House, a small and unusual building, has been the subject of several topographical artists including Thomas Allom, who made a very large record of Westmorland. Coincidentally, the first and most comprehensive exhibition of his work and its supporting catalogue were completed recently. The art of topographical engravings became a business which grew out of the Picturesque movement expounded by Gilpin. After the end of the Napoleonic wars with a settled and more prosperous society, those who could were able to take to the Lakes, and, as we see at Kendal, rented houses for the purpose of exploring the whole region. Defoe, Mrs Gaskell, of this period, Charles Lamb, Coleridge, all told of their expeditions and impressions.

Bridge House is built of stone with a flagged roof and 'wrestler' slates probably in about the sixteenth-century by the Braithwaites of Ambleside Hall. It has been host to many uses and, occupations: as a home, a family of six lived in here. For some time it was used for storing apples, and it may well have been the counting house for the mill further upstream. In 1834 Allom recorded the setting, with tall trees, before a new road to Rydal was built and a new bridge constructed. Earlier the artist William Green, whom Wordsworth patronised (see page 36) and who had an exhibition room in the market place, described Bridge House as being used as a tea room and weaving shop. Later 'Charity' Rigg (he of the six children), who repaired chairs and also made rustic baskets, sold the potted ferns and mosses he made up here; after this antiques were sold, then it was a cobbler, until it eventually became an information centre for the National Trust.

For contemporary work you should visit Ambleside Church which has a study of Mother and Child by that much revered sculptor Josefina de Vasconcellas, now over ninety. Her work can also be seen at Cartmel Priory, Carlisle Cathedral, Rydal Hall and the Oddfellows Gallery in Kendal.

From Ambleside, Townend House is no distance. This yeoman's house is rendered and painted white and contains one of the most accessible collections in situ of vernacular oak carving. There is a quintessential cottage garden approach with a rustic gate. The chimneys are large, round and solid, they serve the house well. Here is a kitchen to surpass any one idea of this style. Every piece, from the open hearth where the range now stands to the buffet, is all of a piece – a seventeenth-century fitted kitchen. There are oak cupboards, one with open spindle front, a sloping desk and a long-case clock, and all slot together with liberal helpings of surface decoration or carving carried out by several generations of Brownes; such as the nineteenth-century interlacing and geometric motifs of the cupboard doors by George Browne who also carved the ornate child's chair. It is dark, with oak shutters, chairs and stools and a clean flagged floor, and dark on a dull day but no less appealing.

Its occupiers have conferred a solidity on the house through their occupations and standing in the community. The Brownes held mayoral office, defended the borders, were appointed to high constable, and clerk of works at Berwick Docks, and one a senior canon at Ripon. The last occupant, George, collected and carved and I suspect revered the craft of furniture-making, for which Westmorland was famous.

This was the last stop before Dalemain and the Eden Valley but first there is Kirkstone Pass, so well described by Dorothy Wordsworth with the red amber glow of autumn.

6

Kendal and Longlesddale

Cumbria

If Kendal seems more like a border or frontier town this may be because the River Kent winds around it, and it is more on the edge of the Lakes; Carlisle and Scotland are not far and the town is near Yorkshire and Lancashire. Walking around is a pleasant exercise, and I was struck by the evidence of a serious wool industry. Flemish weavers came to Kendal in the fourteenth century and helped to make it wealthy with the famous Kendal green drugget (cloth). Holy Trinity is the largest parish church in Cumbria, recalling the beautiful wool churches of Suffolk and the Cotswolds. A thousand people could worship. Although much Victorianised it still contains the monument to its famous son, the painter George Romney, who returned and died in Kendal thirty-seven years after he had left his young wife to paint for his fortune.

Kendal must have more yards (alleys) than any other northern town that I have visited, so much so that these are all numbered, for which the local 'posties' need training time to locate. The fine buildings are the legacy of the town's prosperous past. In Highgate on the left, but off the street in a garden and yard, I found the Brewery Arts Centre with a mêlée of real ale tasting, locals meeting, gossiping (there is street called Gossipgate in Alston) and taking lunch, and a small exhibition. The exterior has been quite sensitively converted. Its little café would benefit from some loving care in its next design, but the food is satisfying and served with a welcome, and as far as I could judge mostly made in situ.

Further up Highgate numbers 134-136 are an elegant pair of Georgian houses, with smooth ashlar stone fronts by Francis Webster built on the site of weaving shops. I noted the yards or courts 17, 20, 22, 119, 161 and Highgate Hall, where New Inn Yard makes an interesting townscape. There is a handful of late Victorian shop fronts, a nice deco-ish Woolworth's with the first floor still remaining, and Sands, the sixteenth-century almshouses. These were built in 1659 and have a garden court similar to those in Wells in Somerset. An amusing sign in a nearby yard requests the populace to 'commit no nuisance'.

Continuing on this side I saw at the end of another yard a neat Georgian building with an outside stair which was originally the Shakespeare Theatre of 1829. Edmund Keane performed here. Sadly, it lasted only five years or so in the face of opposition from Quakers and temperance groups, and although used as a ballroom for many years, poverty eventually forced its closure in the early nineteenth-century. Yet this tale has a happier ending. In 1992 it was converted to a church, a complete volte face as many churches are converted into arts centres.

Some of the yards remind one of Edinburgh, for on the west side of the street they have such a drop that hand rails are need-ed to take you down towards the river. Some courts are so narrow that they barely seem to exist and others are so dark they can hardly be seen. The building that leads from the entrance of the fine fronted number 188 has a fanlight worth seeing, and court 189 next to the brewery is the finest of all. Of shops, Farrers coffee shop is one of the oldest specialist food shops in the country, founded in 1819 on an earlier site of 1640. The original Bank of Westmorland, established in 1833, is one of many superior commercial and public buildings. Interesting wrought-iron work in almost art nouveau decoration can be seen in the entrance of number 62, with its white and black pilasters. The latest addition of 1893 to the town hall has a strong French influence, added to Francis Webster's assembly rooms. Earlier it was the White Hall, possibly the exchange rooms where the wool trade with Virginia was transacted.

Almost every building style can be found in Kendal, includ-ing medieval jetties at the Old Fleece Inn, which has columns not dissimilar to the White Bull at Ribchester and the Sun Inn at Kirkby Lonsdale. Finkle Street, which I discovered means elbow, is an old curved shopping street. (I have seen Finkle Streets in most northern towns.) Here Mrs and Mrs Brennan the grocers have set out their wares with flair: pies and sausages in well dressed windows. There is a profusion of local cheeses and the spoils of the damson attended by properly dressed staff, just as grocers used to be. The first-floor windows above the shops should be seen: there are plenty of decorated pediments and cornices. Arthur Simpson, (see page 11) the Kendal craftsman and Quaker, also opened his first shop in Bury's Yard. He was apprenticed to Gillow of Lancaster in the late nineteenth century, had a philosophy of simplicity and followed the Aesthetic movement making church and domestic furniture, which can seen at Abbot Hall Museum.

On the evening of my first visit to Kendal I stayed at a farm in Longsleddale, accessible only down a picturesque winding approach. This leads to the side of the fells which on an early June evening seemed to be paradise. It is barely a hamlet, no more than a few farmhouses and a church and the start of what promised to be a superb walk to Ullswater across an old Roman road. This valley from another world was the inspiration for the nineteenth-century novelist Mrs Humphry Ward and John Cunliffe.

Mr and Mrs Waine, with whom I stayed, have love and respect for the land that has given them a living, providing pasture for their sheep and black cattle. They are now paying back that debt. They have planted 20,000 trees and the heather is growing again at the top of the fell behind the house. And leaving the meadows to the wild flower harvest has produced species some had never seen. Just opposite, on the other side of the valley, I was shown the large upright stones of the former Roman road which went from here up to Carlisle and, one supposes, the Wall. I was given a reminder of the beautiful dale, coming back with a house leek plantlet and seed heads of Welsh poppy in the hope that I might get them to settle down south the following spring.

I have not yet seen the Kendal Museum where the naturalist and master of northern walking, Alfred Wainwright, was the first honorary curator and supporter. I have to return. A week in June spent between here and Cockermouth, looking at the wild flowers, walking, visiting the galleries and winding down, would be one of the most peaceful and relaxing interludes. Indeed, I would like to take advantage of the twice-weekly bus, which other green travellers might like to note, that runs from Kendal through the dale to the head at Sad Gyll, and leave the car. Just walk.

The Pennine Pottery, Alston

Cumbria

There is a sign on the road between Melmerby and Alston
which the wise will heed; it cautions travellers not to take to
this road lightly. Spring arrives late. May can be cold and it is not
uncommon for snow to fall as the winds blow across from the
east, through the Pennine chain.

Imagine this. From Melmerby, after a long climb up Hartside,
a fell of about 2000 feet and one of the highest peaks in the
Pennines, lies Alston, a tightly built town with perching houses,
appearing to hang from the outcrop. Just two miles further on
there is a sign on the right to the Pennine Pottery. Although you
have dropped about 500 feet since Hartside, the height is still
noticeable and the far-reaching fells and horizon-stretching sky
are visually and spiritually restorative. It is high and solitary.

Clargill House is an eighteenth-century single-storey farmhouse on an old drovers' road not afraid to take the weather
head on. Inside, the byre next to the house has been white-
washed. The heartfelt greeting rebuts the bleak setting. The cow
stalls are simply as they were with uneven floors, a table and a set
of chairs in each and piles of magazines, with rugs hanging on
the walls. I was lucky enough to share a table with a pair of regu-
lars who drive from Alston, not just for lunch – they were tucking
into gargantuan bacon and mushroom sandwiches, large enough
to feed you up for the day – but also to buy a loaf of Pennine
Pottery bread. These loaves lend a whole new meaning to that
rather hackneyed term farmhouse loaf. These would feed the
farmer's whole family. On the way to the tea room you may see
Peter Lascelles as he works in his studio next door, where his
Pennine stoneware of a soft, moorland blue, is on view or being
thrown. I have liked the smell of a potter's room ever since I first
experienced that aroma of wet, woody drying racks in the pottery
studio when I was at school.

Lascelles' work is understated, the gentle blue-green colour
speaks for itself and the plant-inspired patterns replicate the flowing lines of his mugs, jugs and dishes. The work accords with the

landscape and environment. Unlike the climate, however, the objects throw no surprises. There is an everlasting quality about it. The wares are functional, usable and eminently take away-able.

As for food, the portions are ample, can also be taken home and have an integrity worthy of this beauteous spot. They prepare a selection of sandwiches as well as the aforementioned bacon, mine made with the famed bread had a liberal helping of thick plum chutney, but there is also gooseberry and orange. It is all good and great value, as is the apple pie, probably the best value I have ever encountered. As usual I took a slice away for the next leg of my journey to Northumberland. Others will succumb to the treacle tart, shortbread or chocolate cake and orders can be placed in advance for any of the cakes and, of course, one of those bumper loaves.

Communicating and sharing, just how I would best describe this open-hearted working and creative home. The Lascelles invite all, even those on horseback who can tether their steeds in the field, to enjoy the aesthetic and human qualities of hand thrown pottery and hand-prepared food.

The map shows that the topography of Hartside, although the Eden Valley is a green sandwich between the Lakeland fells, is an indomitable and uninhabited fragment of the Pennine chain. But there are some hamlets and farmsteads, even among these fells, through which Alfred Wainwright traversed in 1938. In his own witty style he thanked the motorists for driving the walker into the high places, yet his description of that epic trek really makes mine, a mere motorist's recollections, sound wimpish.

I enjoyed my time in Alston, ferreting in the antique shop, buying fruit and looking at the lanes; a grey town, of millstone grit, it is very cheek by jowl-ish. Alston is an early industrial town founded on the wealth of the lead mines, and subsequently suffered when cheap imported lead arrived in the late nineteenth century. Many of the shops have their original facades, the greengrocers on the market square, for example, whose wonderful sign – thank goodness they saved it – shows that it was once the cycle shop.

The Village Bakery, Melmerby, and the Eden Valley

Cumbria

Anyone visiting the Eden Valley will do well at any time, but especially in the autumn when this flourishing valley is matched by the food and welcome at the Village Bakery in Melmerby. Here the long triangular village green reminds one that the local farmers had to corral their cattle and defend themselves against marauders. There is a sixteenth-century red sandstone church, and it is not far from Little Salkeld, where Long Meg and her daughters, an ancient ring of red, smooth standing stones, looks outwards to the Pennines in the east and the Lake fells in the west. Nearby are Lacy's caves, a set of small 'rooms' carved out in sandstone – reputedly by a master mason whom Sir Richard Lacy brought back from the Crusades – have arches, all with perfect symmetry.

Melmerby had its own place in the Border raids or Riever history, and is the last village before you drive up Hartside. It is known for a natural phenomenon called the Helm, a very strong wind that gusts down from the Pennines through here and other villages nearby, although many places are unaffected. Melmerby's situation means that it takes the full force of the Helm. This might happen once or twice a year and is linked to the equinoxes. Like the Mistral it blows and wanes in two days or so. Locals are able to tell when it is coming as a white cloud called the Helm Bar hangs above Hartside and the immediate neighbourhood becomes still. It travels east and the houses that face the Pennines have tiny windows to reduce the impact.

The Village Bakery is the perfect epicurean antidote for travellers, a comforting port in any storm. It was opened by Andrew Whitley, who first set up his nationally known wood- fired bakery in 1976, in a converted eighteenth-century stone barn. Be prepared to be carried away by the quality of the food prepared in this out-of-the-way village. On my first visit, a long-awaited pilgrimage for good food, I had travelled from the Lakes via Townend and on the second, via the Roman wall through other villages in the Eden Valley. Arriving late on both occasions I was still nourished, engulfed with kindness and encouraged to relax.

The Bakery is a mecca for organic or taste seekers and as food shops and village restaurants go, this one is genuine. They are not fazed by late arrivals; as long as they have something to offer you, they serve and you can eat. The tea room and the bakery behind face the village green. The shop is small, and you are aware of food being prepared in the kitchen next door to the tables. Sacks of flour and organic potatoes sit on the slate shop floor reminding one that produce is grown on a five-acre small-holding behind the bakery. I have eaten high tea and breakfast and bought their distinguished bread. Every morsel oozes with taste. A deep flan is served with fresh salad, real leaf tea and comforting bread and butter. The quality of the ingredients is the key to each dish or baking and much is local. The coffee is roasted in Carlisle, the dry-cured hams from Richard Woodhall in Millom, all, but positively all, the bread and cakes are made with organic flour milled traditionally either from Shipton Mill in Gloucestershire or stone-ground at Little Salkeld. They bake Borrowdale tea bread with rye, marvellous for those with wheat allergies; among the temptations for the sweet tooth are Westmorland parkin, Grasmere gingerbread, date slices, fruit and carrot cakes, scones and, naturally, Cumberland rum butter.

I propose that you plan your excursions to Brampton, Carlisle or Penrith so that you can dip into the unbeatable breakfasts, lunches and teas. For breakfast, raspberry porridge, with cream and honey or oak-smoked Inverawe kippers with buttered bread are served with free-range eggs or cinnamon pancakes as well as noble hams and bacon. At lunch, there might be carrot and orange soup, bean casserole or grilled Cumberland sausages washed down with some organic cider or wine, ale or perry. Open sandwiches or trenchers flaunt their weight of smoked trout or organic roast pork, and with puddings such as plum brûlée or Cumberland rum nicky with small portions of home-made trenchers for children, everyone is considered.

From Melmerby I journeyed north-eastward to Alston and Hexham and visited Kirkoswald, further up the valley, where the village shopkeeper was especially helpful and sells most of the day-to-day needs. Kirkoswald has long narrow streets running down to the Eden and a rather odd church with its campanile detached from the main body. The college, stylishly built in 1696, reminded me of the grammar school at Appleby Magna in Leicestershire. It is now a private house, but the crenellated wall and gatehouse and a large walled garden can be seen from the road. It has nine bays, two projecting wings and very early sash windows, perhaps making it one of the earliest examples of classical architecture in the North.

I travelled to Brampton to see the architect Philip Webb's church, St Martin's, with its unusual barrel-vaulted aisles, and gem-like colours in the stained glass designed by Edward Burne-Jones and executed by William Morris. This a rare church, almost square, in a deep pink sandstone from Wetheral quarry, consecrated in 1878. The internal roof styles consist of a transverse vaulted ceiling in the north aisle, a lean-to effect painted in the south aisle and flat in the nave itself. Green Lane, one of his precious domestic houses, still stands (most have been destroyed) outside the town, with a truly asymmetrical Webb facade.

At Wetheral Priory Gate House, the remains of a twelfth century Benedictine cell for twelve monks from St Mary's in York which later became part of the vicarage are almost in the farmyard; you climb the tight winding stairs to a large room with an oriel window and good views of the valley. The road to Armathwaite runs along the Carlisle to Settle line where the viaducts are monumental works of engineering in their own right. This one is 100ft high with 80ft spanning arches, built between 1830 and 1834; a road worth taking when the trees are still in full leaf in October, because it is such a sheltered valley.

At the bend in the road outside Armathwaite just over the river, where excellent salmon and trout are to be fished, you will see one of the Eden benchmarks. These are a collection of sculptures set along the river valley depicting and interpreting life and the environment. Two large pieces of sandstone, a large fish and a minnow appear to nestle close like mother and child and are large enough to sit on and give a view. This is sculpture in the landscape which crystallises its setting of the gentle valley and the sandy-coloured fields.

Wordsworth House and Cockermouth

Cumbria

Every visitor to Cumbria should put Cockermouth on his list. It was one of many towns studied in the 1970s and found deserving enough of conservation. Its architectural and archaeological legacy is secured. Although many former mills have been transformed, the character of the town, with its fine buildings, is still apparent. The main street, justly so-called, is where the statue of the Earl of Mayo looms large in the middle of a wide and tree-lined thoroughfare, off which any number of garths, or alleyways, run down to what was once another life of Cockermouth, a busy, noisy mill town.

The houses are awash with colour and are attractions in themselves. Each owner uses a bright colour to highlight the building features, even purple. You can see windows framed in emerald and lime green, others where the white makes a lively contrast with an ochre wash. And they seem to be just as proud of the backs; take the case of Albion Yard. One house has a glowing marine-blue wash, white window frames and a blue door. Like Kendal, with fewer hills, the individual quality comes from the snickets or alleys which run everywhere. One leads from the car park to the small quiet market; this was first granted its charter in 1221. I found a fishmonger selling dressed crabs, monkfish and herrings, a vegetable and flower stall. The number of hotels and carriage yards confirm that Cockermouth was both a market and trading town and industry thrived here in the last century. The town still trades, less frenetically I imagine, and even with a fair share of visitors, delighting in the useful shops, pubs and buildings it is difficult to imagine an overcrowded Cockermouth.

Wordsworth House, famed as William Wordsworth's birth place, is an excellent starting point for a walk, then along Main Street, over the bridge, always looking up to the left and right towards the castle. Cockermouth held a powerful position: it once connected Cumberland and Northumberland. The Percy family owned the castle until 1670 when it became a garrison during the Scottish border raids. It was rebuilt in about 1135; it switched from one side to another in the Wars of the Roses, and escaped Civil War damage, passing into the Wyndham family's hands. And perhaps the fact that Cockermouth was once in Scotland explains its affinity with some of the wide-street border towns. In common with other settlements the siting of the town at the confluence of the Derwent and the Cocker tells the story. Most of the industrial buildings are on the north side near the Derwent which flows in front of the castle ruins. There were as many as forty working mills at the height of the town's success in the nineteenth century.

The Brewery, founded at Lorton in 1828 by the Jennings family, still brews and uses the same source of water from a well that the Normans used earlier. And this family-run company still owns many of the friendly hostelries in this town and elsewhere in the North. It is difficult to imagine, for example, that hundreds of people were employed to make hats; there were tanneries, dye works, cotton and linen mills, and others produced bobbins. Unfortunately all the products, including the cotton and linen that were manufactured here, have been superseded by man-made fabrics and new fashions. The picture that Mr Bradbury paints in one of his excellent little books on the town is colourful, of looms weaving gingham cotton checks, as well as the spinning of wool.

Banks the locksmith, established in 1836, is my choice of emporium, unmissable with a large key hanging above the front door. Inside, the original wide mahogany counters are still used, as are the rows of boxes behind, labelled in gold lettering with the words dolly pegs, scale weights and nails. Banks has that very special aroma of hardware. At the back is a wonderful door leading into Banks Court, from where staff went to the mill. It shows how houses and their burgage plots became small workshops, with mills and factories at the rear. But there are other proper shops selling shoes, books, bread and confectionery, as well as the tweed and hosiery-focused windows of the gentlemen's outfitters.

The town hall now houses the tourist information centre, a well set-up place. Cocker House, a Quaker meeting house in Kirkgate, is worth looking at and the old court house has pilasters and interesting windows. Down the court to the side of Banks an old tannery has interesting cast-iron window frames with red rose centres, and opposite is the Toy Museum, which should be given the accolade of the museum most off the urban beaten track.

Nikolaus Pevsner calls Wordsworth House 'a swagger house'. It lives up to this description in position, colour and size. The house lies behind a rather attractive stone wall with an arching curve above the gate leading to the entrance steps which frame the portico. The entrance is important, the proportion is right with three bays; the stone quoins and the terracotta wash all give a fine appearance. Even the rear deserves examination: neat with some attractive cross-banded lead pipes. The house came via the Sheriff of Cumberland to the estate of Sir James Lowther, for whom John Wordsworth was agent, hence his son William's birth-place. It is an extremely friendly house.

Some features are especially attractive; take for example the different tile surrounds in the fireplaces in each room, nine-teenth-century in the parlour with a hearth surround made in Liverpool in about 1750. The south-facing bedroom has another attractive fireplace with alternating tiles of duck-egg blue and caramel with a raised apple design on the last; this is repeated in the ante-room, with a posy of flowers instead. Another has deli-cate apple-green tiles also with a raised motif design.

Plasterwork takes precedence in the reception rooms. The drawing room was given an embellishment with a series of stepped Corinthian pilasters either side of the fireplace as well as ornate scroll pediments above the doors. The dining room with plaster carving has a satisfying scale with a view across the street and up to the church. It is worth pausing to enjoy the view from the panelled landing to the garden where Wordsworth played.

In the parlour one finds Leeds creamware and contemporary etchings of the Lakes, attracting followers of the Picturesque, and as many as forty views published in 1821 by William Green of Ambleside (see page 24), a friend of Wordsworth who was also his patron. A grander forerunner of our picture postcards. The small reading room invites to you to pause and look at the family por-traits. Lastly, in the ante-room, hang fine pen and wash drawings, contemporary with the house, by Edward Dayes, softly done, of, among others, Grasmere and Windermere.

Warm, local and dedicated staff make the whole visit enjoyable. The tea room, where the staff wear aprons made with calico from a National Trust working mill, is decidedly devoted to the visitors' comfort and enjoyment. Possibly one of the small-

est, it is unequivocally, one of the most congenial. The manager cooks and acquires everything locally, even vegetables from the kitchen garden. Fresh scones, gingerbread shortbread and Borrowdale tea bread are superior in quality and their puddings, which vary with the season, are prepared with local fruit such as blackberries in their full flush.

To set the scene: from a service passage you enter the kitchen where food is cooked and arranged. Just one small table for visitors is here, another room has about a dozen seats; the former is my favourite, near the small glass-topped table replete with home baking. This situation recalls the bonhomie of friends sitting at the kitchen table gossiping while one cooks. It was the original kitchen with cast-iron range, ham hooks and a drying rack. Today's jars of lentils and nuts add colour and echo the tones of the warm quarry-tiled floor. It is not difficult to imagine Lakeland teas: the high teas of chicken, ham, lobster and salmon with cakes and tea being served here in the past. Here is good homely food with a dresser bearing blue plates and meat dishes in a neat fashion. Their thick chunky soups are made with tomato, carrot, celery and lentils and thick sandwiches are prepared to order. Some of the jams are unusual, with the choice depending on who gives what or what is growing: gooseberry mixed with elderberry flower sounded good to me. This tea room quashes those who too easily say 'we haven't the room to cook'. This is the proof that space is less of a problem than attitude.

Outside bees were humming in the walled garden, which was filled with poppies, foxgloves, delphiniums and peonies. If you want to sit and ponder the influence that this garden had on one of the greatest English romantic poets there is time and space. Wordsworth was indeed much favoured in his birthplace.

LANCASHIRE

Clitheroe and Garstang

Lancashire

In the nicest possible way, Clitheroe resembles a lovely mixed bag of old-fashioned northern sweets such as you can buy at the sweet shop in King Street: pear or sarsaparilla drops and lemon sherbets. But Clitheroe has the odd surprise in the form of architecture at the bottom of the bag. It is unpretentious, unspoilt and unreservedly down to earth. The town parades its proper, useful shops and elegant Georgian buildings.

My first visit to this market town coincided with a summer folk weekend. The music drifted up to the church and around the streets as I avoided the showers. I came upon groups of black faces at every turn – people or morris folk painted up, not my favourite Swaledale sheep. They were disconcerting, yet amusing as they were carrying besoms, were covered in bells and sported long-handled mops with woolly heads. Folk here means morris men and women, as well as strings, brass and pipes.

Clitheroe sits on a plateau in the Ribble Valley not far from Pendle Hill, with its two high points making its position one of its best assets. The church at one end was built in the twelfth century and Victorianised in 1861 and has an exceptional view down over the town roofs. The remains of a Norman castle at the opposite end of the town, supposedly one of the smallest in England, is now surrounded by a public park. Even this is rather played down. I started my perambulation near the church which has a large number of table memorials; these are stones on supports rather than being set upright.

For the architecturally curious there are courts, alleys and houses to investigate and study. There is a pleasing mixture of Victorian Gothic and late Georgian houses on Church Street, now occupied by solid solicitors, some of these houses have quite important pediments and all have their own character and different facade, one with Ionic pilasters. Many are decorated in subtle wash. One of the most interesting houses is the black and white house next to the church with a plaque high up giving the date of 1808, and around the corner a handsome lead rain pipe of 1757. An amusing town hall built in the 1860s with a Gothic revivalist influence stands next to a building, with a crenellated porch which is now a bank. At the bottom of the street is the White Lion, a confection of a nineteenth-century copy of seventeenth-century gabled ends, robust windows with an archway leading to the stables of a former coaching inn. Castle Street also has its share of original shop fronts, mostly nineteenth-century; one really takes the eye with its grape decoration and complicated pediments and scrolls all in plaster. These are picked out in purple and contrast with the green and cream background.

The sumptuous gold lettering outside the late nineteenth-century White Horse Hotel shows that the nineteenth-century merchants pandered a little to the style of the times; it stands proud, quite literally, a flamboyant three-dimensional sign. There are too few reminders of these once bustling hotels; how pleasing that the newt and magpie pub fashion has not reached Clitheroe. But I also applaud Clitheroe's unpainted face, its different levels and buildings, based on the fortunes of agriculture and cotton.

I discovered that Clitheroe had been a truly patriotic borough. In 1897 great efforts were made to celebrate Queen Victoria's jubilee in style, I read an account from the book Clitheroe In Its Railway Days which showed that there was every manifestation of loyalty. Copious committees were formed, energetic preparations made, gigantic schemes and a huge bonfire and magnificent rockets were all planned and successfully executed. Even the castle keep was decorated with gorgeous lights to present a fairy-like scene, where monster bonfires on Whalley Nab illuminated the whole town in a collective celebration taking place over several days. Every one entered the processions, schoolchildren, local soldiers and of course the mayor and aldermen. Three hundred and sixty people were given a special dinner of roast beef (what else?) and plum pudding, albeit in midsummer. There was beer for the men and a quarter of pound of tea for each woman with tobacco and snuff for those who cared for it. The mayor and aldermen were attentive to a fault sending the elder people home, 'brimful of jubilant and grateful thoughts'.

I made a link with today's illustrious sausage shop, Cowmans, and with Councillor Cowman who in that celebratory year provided a great ox from Scotland for a large roasting and where those who carved the ox had their names recorded. The roast was so popular that they ran out of meat. Morris-men also took part in the mile-long procession containing a representative from every possible group, and the writer noted that 'in no town in England were there more effective displays of loyalty than in the right royal borough of Clitheroe'.

Cowman's has a pleasant facade with its incised gold lettering on a green-blue slate front and a proud proclamation is that their sausages contain 'no slurry slurp or goo, just quality meat'. And you know it must be so. The sausages include honey pork, sage and onion pork, Clitheroe hot and spicy pork, Lancashire pork, pork and tarragon and so on. I think there are as many as fifty-six different combinations of the banger. Cowmans is no longer in the same family as the Mr Cowman who procured the ox, but it has presence in the town and sticks to what it does well, just sausages.

Walter Greenwood, who wrote Love On The Dole, grew up in and described the real depression of the thirties; his childhood memories, not surprisingly, include food. One of his treats was an extraordinary combination of hot black peas topped off with ice cream. It was customary to throw peas, grown so well up here, whole, pod and all, into a fire. I find it hard to imagine the ice cream topping. My peas rarely used to get past the allotment gates, cooking them seems sacrilegious.

The troubles of the Greenwood family were those that beset many mill workers, whose diet of bread, tea, porridge and the odd piece of bacon was the superior version of the norm, tea, bread and porridge. Lancashire food history is very much bound up with the hours that housewives had to work. Slow cooking of cheap joints and offal was usual while the mother was working, or in some cases where there was no room to cook she used the pie shop. All over this area, in the markets and the streets, that heritage lives on. Hot pie shops still have large displays to tempt today's tourist. This tradition was born out of a basic need, the mill workers' long hours, early breakfast and a hungry family waiting for food. But the hot pie shop kept everyone happy and the housewife could buy the supper on the way home.

For sweet treats the Chocolate Box in Clitheroe has its original mahogany counters. The window shelves carry dishes of sugared almonds, all types of chocolates, toffee, with a penny-in-the-slot Fry's chocolate bar and some fine examples of chocolate box design. Traditional sweets are still manufactured here.

Clitheroe is a prosperous town, with tourism, trade and quarrying. I also found 'those black puddings, split down the middle, plastered with mustard, and thick collops of bacon fat'. From Lancashire up to the Lakes black pudding was offered at farmhouse breakfasts. I did not meet any Goosnargh cakes, not even in Goosnargh, where the Horns Inn offers a wonderful menu of local foods and a black beauty, a Shorrocks Lancashire cheese, unpasteurised which gives the taste. It is encased in black wax and hangs like a witch's cauldron in the bar. I was so taken with this that I bought one from the smallholding where I stayed which just happened to have a spare. You can also buy local cheeses at the market in Clitheroe where the WI market on Tuesdays sells marmalades, jams and pickles, bread, soft fruit and cakes. These markets are a good way to meet the local people and their produce. I found another at Garstang, not far from Clitheroe, an exceptionally friendly market town, bordering the Wyre with a central street and small, elegant covered market. The main street is a pleasant walk and was decorated with bright banners denoting all the principal families and there is a quite charming arts centre set up in a restored school where anyone can meet to gossip, take coffee and see a fine array of local art work.

So what happens in Clitheroe today? The Platform Gallery shows a wide range of contemporary art. And the town supports many active groups; there are organised evening walks into the country and an up-to-the-minute sculpture trail begun by their artist in residence, Thompson Dagnall, whose work is inspired by the landscape and the people who work it.

11

Gawthorpe Hall, Burnley

Lancashire

A tactile and textural story is woven through this house from the seventeenth-century wood carving and plasterwork, the nineteenth-century furniture and patterned encaustic tiles to a magnificent collection of needlework and textiles. This is Gawthorpe Hall's distinction. And the textile collection still grows, accommodated in a house which has survived changes and was threatened by development.

Gawthorpe stems from a favourite period, the late seventeenth century. It is attributed to Robert Smythson, who designed Hardwick Hall in Derbyshire and Wollaton Hall just outside Nottingham. The material is sandstone with that soot-worn look of so many northern buildings. Thankfully, adequate land was secured so that the wooded drive contains the house and retains the character of the estate, yet it is almost in Burnley. The elegant, symmetrical south front is compact, Elizabethan on the cusp of Jacobean style with three projecting bays.

Most of the alterations are interior, other than the porch and the second floor balustrade, with magnificent nineteenth-century decorations made by Sir James Barry between 1849 and 1852. The contemporary contribution which makes Gawthorpe so engaging is a remarkable collection of embroidery and needlework accumulated by the last member of the Shuttleworth family to live here. The Hon Rachel Kay-Shuttleworth left this as a living archive. She wanted it to be a 'craft house'.

Gawthorpe was built by the Shuttleworth family, whose lineage can be traced to the late thirteenth century. This is depicted on a wooden panel in the hall where early family members and their descendants' initials are carved with dates between 1443 and 1604. This family made good marriages, increasing their wealth and position. Sir Richard Shuttleworth inherited a fortune, was a successful barrister and Chief Justice in Chester with estates in Westmorland and Yorkshire. He decided in 1596 to rebuild the house, but died in 1599 before building commenced. His younger brother, the Reverend Lawrence, who held a living in Warwickshire, finished the project; perhaps he encountered Robert Smythson and his work in the Midlands before he moved here. He in turn did not leave a direct heir, but his nephew Richard with stylish patronage brought the place alive with art and music when he inherited in 1606. The accounts reveal that the Hall rang with the sound of plays and even circuses. Richard's social, professional and political standing were progressed and he lead the Parliamentarians at the Civil War Battle of Whalley.

The Shuttleworth line adopted the name Kay-Shuttleworth on a marriage in 1842, and a period of significant changes began. Dr James Phillips Kay who married Janet Shuttleworth, the heiress, was a friend of the architect Charles Barry, whom he asked to alter and improve the house and estate in 1849. It was during this period that Charlotte Brontë visited and recorded that she liked the house. Gawthorpe was ultimately given to the National Trust in 1970 with, most importantly, the textile collection of Rachel Kay-Shuttleworth, the last member of the family to reside at Gawthorpe. This is shown beautifully and used as a reference for students of textiles, craft and design.

One of the first rooms in the tour, after passing through the entrance hall, is the dining room; altered by Barry in 1852, it has the original galleried screens, indeed those which would have given actors and performers their entrance or wings. Today the sideboards replace the former small projecting stage and a strong retro-Elizabethan feel is supported by Pugin's design for the Crace curtains and wallpaper – double flock – drawing reference from sixteenth-century Italian designs and similar to Lord Irvine's notorious wallpaper in the House of Lords. In addition to the textiles, pictures from the National Portrait Gallery hang on matching cord, a seventeenth-century fashion which complements the wallpaper. Devotees of the craft of Gillow of Lancaster's furniture-making will find examples of their chairs and tables. In the drawing room eye-catching carved plaster work, ceiling and the oak panelling are the original Jacobean, the panelling by the same craftsmen who made the screen in the dining room. Both are ornate and unusual, a mastery of material and craftsmanship. The centre row of panels has a semi-circle carved in relief, and where each panel meets its neighbour there is also a column in relief. The ceiling accentuates the panelling, abutting with a superb carved cornice of pomegranates and leaves. Jewel-bright Crace furnishings, carpet and curtains, and a specially designed ornate teapoy in burr-walnut for storing tea caddies by Pugin for Janet Kay-Shuttleworth give this room its nineteenth-century overlay. The long gallery is very much of the seventeenth century, an elegant room for taking exercise and similar to the gallery at Ham House in Surrey, Aston Hall in Birmingham or Hardwick Hall. But Gawthorpe has more pendent plasterwork than the former and an intricate plaster frieze by Thomas and Francis Gunby.

The sampler collection is just one element of primarily British eighteenth and nineteenth-century needlework. This forms an introduction to the exhibition with more than 500 items from a total collection of 14,000 pieces. There are, however, some modern surprises such as a Jean-Paul Gaultier and Christian Lacroix outfit. Some pieces are quite outstanding, and really worth travelling for. The Hungarian and Balkan hats stick in the mind, the African shanty hat woven in cotton cloth, everyday objects are given more meaning through the style and quality of the work: scarves, red leggings and slippers, sewing bags, all with their stitched symbolism. There is denim in all its shades, some appliquéd some with cut out lace giving examples from every corner and culture of the textile world. Rachel Kay-Shuttleworth was not just a collector but also practitioner.

Modern oak cases show off these beautiful artefacts to their best advantage, cases designed in Arts and Crafts style, in particular that of C F A Voysey, honouring the movement Rachel admired. One of the most charming pieces is a long white full-buttoned coat made for a child in 1925, recalling the care which used to be taken in making children's clothes. Another coat, of 1876, is in fine cotton rep, the front covered with embroidery, and with a delightful collar and unusual side pockets. A little navy knitted French orphanage jacket and a hand knitted collarless Austrian jacket caught my eye as did some delicate primavera organdie. Gawthorpe is a melting pot of craft and social history, even down to the tea cosy collection.

Charlotte Brontë made several visits; the first was in 1850 when she found it 'grey, stately and picturesque'. After she was married she visited again in 1855, having also spent some time with Sir James Kay-Shuttleworth in the Lakes at the same time as her biographer Mrs Gaskell; Charlotte's husband was offered the living which a new church built on land given by the Shuttleworths would provide, but this was declined and she was not to visit again as she died in the same year.

Lancashire hospitality certainly earns its reputation in the tea room at Gawthorpe Hall. The ladies give you their attention in an impressive, simply restored estate building across the courtyard

with an outside staircase. They wait your pleasure in a spacious room with an impressive cast-iron fireplace and attractive glass light fittings; even for the last straggling visitors they make sure that, gasping for tea, they are not disappointed. The fresh soup is maybe leek and potato or pea and mint in the summer. Just as you would expect on the menu are cheese and onion pie, Lancashire hotpot, meat and potato pie and vegetables such as leeks, beans, spinach and beetroot from the garden. Fresh green checked cloths on the tables brighten the room which has pleasant mullioned windows. Tea is not served in the courtyard, but they will happily help those who cannot manage the stairs. Permanent outdoor seating for those who cannot walk up would be a boon. You can indulge in cakes such as moist barnbrack, scones, ginger sponge, apple pie, chocolate and walnut and date and walnut cake. Egg curd tart, carrot cake, Bakewell tart, Sad cakes and almond madeira cake come with excellent tea.

Outside in the grounds there are many Barry touches as he completely redesigned the gardens: encaustic tiles on the steps and a parterre of which the Reverend Whitaker, who visited in 1818, would have approved. He felt there was a need of 'light external objects' which the height of the window sills in the house excluded; Barry's parterre in the south garden, now covered with lawn, would have given another Tudory dimension and the pattern a greater depth of view. From the front of the house a series of terraces, some formal in parterre form, with golden and green sculptured box, some less formal, lead the eye to a finial-topped wall. Then the aspect moves over to Pendle.

12

Pendle Heritage Centre, Barrowford

Lancashire

Pendle Heritage Centre contrasts stylishly with the received image of many other heritage centres built in the 1980s. This building, or rather buildings, and the manner of the renovation are completely absorbing; together with the exuberant herb and vegetable garden, well presented shop and tea room, it is a relaxing yet vibrant local attraction.

Park Hill House constitutes the centre itself; it is three pieces of an architectural jigsaw which the exhibition helps to complete. The curators have set out to resolve some of the complicated development of the house which gave me a better insight into the history of this area. Many of the local houses are built in sandstone and gritstone, as opposed to the rendered limestone which you see in Clitheroe. Park Hill is situated in an early industrial village, Barrowford, about five miles from Pendle Hill, a long whale back which reaches out almost to Yorkshire, skirting the Leeds and Liverpool canal. Although of Lancashire in building style, decoration and furniture making, there are marked cross-overs with Yorkshire styles.

Park Hill was in ruins in 1978 when with the help of many charitable bodies it was restored and is now ably managed by the Lancashire Heritage Trust. Much of the house dates back to a seventeenth-century yeoman's hall; it was, however, originally built in about 1460 with three bays, a thatched roof, wattle and daub walls and perhaps a solar. Another stone building or crossing was added at right angles in 1590 with a stone roof, when the then owner Mr Henry Bannister became wealthier. He also added a grand chimney breast to the side, replacing the smoke hole in the roof. As the wool trade thrived, the succeeding owners, even more upwardly mobile, added a Palladian exterior to the early seventeenth-century facade. So the third and fourth stages included an extension to the 1580 crossing, the original thatched house was demolished and then a grander facade and jettied porch were added.

Most of the elegant work was completed in the Georgian period – delicate glazing bars, a pediment and pilasters at the front door – and a more genteel way of life encouraged smaller halls and rooms with first-floor fireplaces for comfort. John Parker Swinglehurst built the Palladian facade in 1780, taking on new ideas but with insufficient space to emulate the grander houses; so the normal proportions were foreshortened and the pediments are squashed without any fanlights. As many as six Palladian houses were developed in this neighbourhood, but there are no great houses here such as Sledmere and Bolton Abbey with their large estates (see pages 89 and 134).

From 1710 the Bannisters lived at Park Hill and the Swinglehursts at Lower Park Hill, two houses which may have formed a very early pair of semi-detached houses for two families; these buildings take a little understanding. The development of the house from 1590 to 1788 is now clearly set out showing its intriguing architecture and archaeology. The spaces have been used imaginatively to display and highlight the area's history; on the staircase good prints of other Lancashire houses enhance the context. Careful and sensitive restoration, especially of paint scrapings, revealed pale blue and rose paint and plaster which have been copied. In between the two houses as I went upstairs I first saw an elegant Venetian window, even better outside where the conjunction of both buildings is also clearer. Park Hill makes a wonderful architectural visit.

A splendid oak door, removed from Rochdale, is just one of several examples of this region's carving. Carpenters' marks can be deciphered and the furniture collection has some exciting work, for example a carved settle with diamond lozenge and scroll patterns. Some of the best furniture was made in West Yorkshire and bought in Leeds by the successful yeoman farmers and cloth maunfacturers, whose fortunes expanded when the Pendle forest was felled from the sixteenth century onwards. These carved chests were important multi-functional pieces, for both sitting on and storing in, and were a prelude to the exceptional furniture I was to see throughout this county and Cumbria. Towneley Hall Art Gallery and Museum also has a fine collection of seventeenth-century regional furniture.

Several displays put the nineteenth-century cotton industry

into context; spinning took place in the south of the county, weaving and some spinning here in the north around Burnley, Nelson and Colne. Naturally one finds a display given over to the famous story of the Pendle witches. For folklore followers there is a witches' trail which leads you through the Trough of Bowland, a wonderful route I took the following day to Lancaster where the witches were hung. The importance of the markets at Clitheroe and Blackburn is interpreted, and that of the Quaker movement led by George Fox; non-conformist chapels are prolific in the North. The beginnings and impact of the Co-operative movement in Rochdale are also here.

There is just enough space devoted to the early settlers – Vikings and Normans – of what was formerly called Blackburnshire; Blackburn was the capital of a Saxon hundred (shire, or administrative sub division) once covered in trees. The change of focus from a single town to many other smaller centres which coincided with the Industrial Revolution becomes clearer here. The townships, however, were as fervent and patriotic as Clitheroe when it came to celebrating royal events; there was no actual castle but they constructed crenellated floats and spent large sums to make sure their processions were as good as any. Cotton is no longer the king it was then, yet there is still a towel-weaving company nearby. Is this one of the last reminders of the loom-weaving industry which made Lancashire?

Pendle's pleasant tea room and shop – visitors and merchandise spill out in an organised fashion – spreads out into a tiny courtyard, an overflow for fine days, where a handful of seats are set among the plants, of which some are for sale. There is also a conservatory area with an enchanting view of a perfect little walled garden. A cruck barn houses a small menagerie of pigs, goats and chickens; something for children to enjoy. There is also a country trail. Here you can partake of a good tea against a pleasant background of conversation.

Tea at Pendle offers good choices, with Chorley cakes, Eccles cakes made with flaky pastry or Sad cakes. And for lunch the hot dishes are equally unpretentious and substantial: bean casserole, cooked gammon, Lancashire hotpot, meat and potato pies and fish pie on a Friday. The keen young chef liaises with the

gardener to keep the kitchen well supplied with own-grown vegetables, fruit and herbs from the walled garden or greenhouse. Asparagus and peas are all grown organically as well as salads, tomatoes, leeks, raspberries and gooseberries for pavlovas in the summer.

In the winter their puddings 'go down well': sticky toffee pudding, banana and cream pie and good old-fashioned apple sponge. Not prepared to rest on their more conventional laurels, they are experimenting with different salads. The couscous and bulgur-based ones, are finding favour. Combined with the relaxing garden, the stone-flagged floor, trug baskets, flowers and stylish grey conservatory, it is a centre that contrives to mix history, archaeology and a regional taste of the good things.

When Celia Fiennes made her journeys across England between 1662 and 1741, she wrote in 1698 about Lancashire and added some strong stuff: 'If all persons, both Ladies, much more Gentlemen, would spend some of their tyme in Journeys to visit their native land, and be curious to inform themselves, and make observations of the pleasant prospects [these included sport, manufacture and buildings], would also form such an idea of England...and cure the evil itch of over-valuing foreign parts.' This equestrian authoress also took advantage of a practice which allowed guests to buy their own meat or fish from markets, which she enjoyed, and then take these victuals to the inn where they were staying to have it cooked. Could we revive this, I wonder?

13

Ribchester Museum and Ribchester

Lancashire

The fisherman I saw on the way to Waddington and Clitheroe gracefully casting out over the Ribble, surely for salmon, made a tranquil and serene picture. Cliché? Maybe, but authentic here. For this river, with wide flowing waters, nourishes the pasture that produces some of the best crumbly creamy cheeses in the country, and has a reputation for good fishing.

I enjoy the town of Ribchester's intimate relationship with water, the river nearby at every turn, bordered by willow and hawthorn. Ribchester is a one-off with a powerful story; like some of its neighbours there is industry and weaving. But this was a Roman town, sited and built by Agricola on a six-acre site in about AD70 as a double-aspect vantage and meeting point in the river bend. It was a crossing point between Roman roads northeast to Yorkshire and north west to Lancashire and on to Carlisle. From this beautiful, low-lying valley there are views to Pendle Hill, cloud-covered on the morning I arrived.

Ribchester has a completeness of scale, it is unchanged and the buildings are intact. It is, as Nikolaus Pevsner labels it in his Buildings of England 'a nice little village'; a vernacular-style weaving village. Yet, where the church now stands may have once stood Bremetennacum (the Roman fort). Medieval recyclers made the most of the Roman materials when they built the church and eighteenth-century builders rescued columns, possibly part of the temple, that form a delightful arcade outside the White Bull pub in the village built above the Roman town.

The tiny museum, somewhat out of character in early twentieth-century village hall style was founded by a Miss Greenall (related to the large Northern brewery family) and explains the contrast between the Roman settlement and the Celtic tribes which followed. That morning it was almost filled by an eager school party avidly hanging on to the curator's words. The original of the famous bronze helmet discovered in 1796 is now in the British Museum – you will only find the replica here – but the pottery, coins, and fragments of a hypercaust make a fascinating accumulation of artefacts. I particularly admire the delicacy of the Roman jewellery (the Museum of Antiquities in Newcastle has a wonderful collection). But Ribchester also holds some exquisite pieces: a pair of delicate tweezers, a fibula, brooches and tiny oil-burning lamps. Of all the remains, for me a replica writing tablet and styli seemed most flawless and covetable.

Many historians in search of antiquities have visited Ribchester; the sixteenth-century traveller John Leland commented on the number of antique coins and stones that he found, and as you walk across the churchyard towards the Norman church with its Norman altar you cannot help speculating upon the other Roman evidence lying under your feet. I rather agree with Walter Greenwood in his book on Lancashire that it would have been wonderful to see more excavation. But how amazed those eighteenth-century villagers must have been when they discovered the treasure they had been living above.

At the east end the church has long windows with, like so many others in this region, boxed pews dated between 1735 and 1761. The tower is squat, and the small close is surrounded by yews. In between the stones the mortar is thick and dark, a regional style, and Lancashire names such as Sidebottom and Greenwood are remembered on the gravestones. Naturally the site has been eroded by time, but the Roman bath house, a short walk around the river bend, is worth seeing. Whether you take this route or another over damp fields in front of a row of cottages, these archaeological remains are at the bottom of a garden. Ribchester is well kept, almost desirable, especially the houses with original windows. I believe the Romans would approve of the neat streets of weavers' cottages.

You see plenty for your time in Ribchester, for only a few hundred metres away at Stydd I found a small group of enchanting classically inspired almshouses with an elegant curving staircase to the first floor loggia or arcade, allowing each resident their own entrance door. These were built by John Shireburn in 1748 for five needy women and a schoolmistress, who relied on neighbours to draw the water they needed from a well in the garden. There are five bays, three central arches with Tuscan central connecting columns, possibly built at the same time as the White

Bull, and again, using the Roman masonry. This delightful building justifies Pevsner's descriptions as 'curious and engaging'. The roofs are slate, the houses in stone and brick and next door there is another curiosity: a barn-like church of 1789 with fine Gothic pointed windows. St Saviour's is a very small stone medieval church built by the knights of St John. It has late seventeenth-century detailing in the pulpit; was this church part of a crusade or Templar hospital?

The Ribble Valley way is well marked and new developments are not intrusive. The economy is lively and the walking is not strenuous, just the right mixture for urban escapees.

14

Waddington, the Ribble Valley, Slaidburn and Bolton-by-Bowland

Lancashire

Waddington deserves to be included in anyone's list of English villages. It is just a mile from Clitheroe. It is a splendid base from which to explore the Trough of Bowland and rural North Lancashire as well as Slaidburn and Clitheroe itself. Waddington is still an agricultural village, in very rich farming country, where you can talk to farmers in one of the pubs which are of differing character and each attracting its own clientele. One appears to be the watering hole for a local pack of MG vintage car enthusiasts. Although the former smithy is now a house and little remains of the original church, rebuilt nearly 100 years ago except for some late fifteenth-century benches, Waddington has its own royal connection: the Hall reputedly gave Henry VI sanctuary after the Battle of Hexham.

The village straggles informally off the main street with a war memorial, brook, bridges and stone cottages. It has enough to make you pause: the enchanting Coronation gardens, full of blue and pink lupins, bounded by that friendly design of white chain fencing, the flowing water and not least Backfold Cottage. This delightful small hotel can be found on the northern side of the square with houses either side in a tiny cobbled lane. A hanging sign outside the small cream washed cottage, with stone mullions and an intriguing window of dolls, charms passers by. The size implies small rooms which are nevertheless planned for comfort, with fresh linen which Daphne Forbes has bought at Bolton-by-Bowland, and fresh flowers.

Anyone can walk straight into the parlour, staying or not. Being a proper parlour, the dining table is covered with a white cloth. There really was a smell of fresh baked scones at six o'clock. Tea can stretch out here. The souvenirs and brass fairings that Daphne has gathered sit on the mantle shelf and side tables, and a welcoming cup of tea is served on a comfortable sofa. The dish of yellow lemon curd smiling at me from a tray was the first of many homemade curds that I was to taste. Tea is served from a silver pot, with warm scones or homemade cakes; thick and rich chocolate, Bakewell tart or a lemon cheesecake. The portions are liberal, a tea to dream about.

Daphne is a perfectionist; she was born here and knows everything there is to know about the area, what to see and where to eat, as she lectured in hotel management before retiring and was responsible for the scientific elements. Some of her students included the present coterie of bright young chefs. She is tireless in her drive for quality. Her guests want for nothing, and she is open-handed with her breakfasts: large jars of fruit muesli, large jugs of fruit juice, good coffee, damson jam, all the cooked ingredients you could wish for, and a basket of assorted breads. The house and kitchen are immaculate and she cooks and waits in her fresh white apron. The delicate dish of Morecambe Bay shrimps which she bought for me on a trip to Lytham St Anne's was unforgettable. A small feast – but feasts do not necessarily have to be large - with thin slices of bread and butter and lemon. What else?

Dining communally encourages friendships; one guest was an enchanting American drama lecturer who returns to the region where she was born almost annually and contrives to visit all the villages, churches and friends by bus or on foot. Country bus services to Waddington are good; Bolton-by-Bowland on the other hand, is not so easy. At breakfast I met a German farmer promoting the satellite farming monitoring system which helps the regulation of crop spraying. He was visiting a local farmer who joined us. This assembly had, I felt, the ingredients of a short story.

From Waddington I drove to Slaidburn, also once in West Yorkshire before the county boundary changes. The clear summer evening made for a fine walk around the village, with its neat terraced cottages, once home to weavers, and a small public garden. Slaidburn was the meeting place of the Forest of Bowland's ruling body which met at the pub in the centre, Hark to Bounty. The grammar school next to St Andrew's has a well-founded proud air, a generous facade of seven bays and elegant cross windows. It was built in 1717 before the Georgian style arrived here; the porch carries importance with its pediment. Inside the church the rood screen is Jacobean with fine open carving. The pulpit is a three-decker and there are good family box pews such as you might see at Kirkby Malham (see page 119).

The Trough of Bowland is unpeopled and has stone barns and sheep. It is intensely green with few villages except Dunsop Bridge, beyond Slaidburn. The bracken was lime-coloured early in the summer, as the fells were just turning. It is an unequalled panorama as the setting sun casts a wonderful shadow on the forest ahead. Three rivers, the Wyre, Hodder and Ribble, all start their long journeys here, there are healthy-coated cattle, cow parsley at its milky fullness, and the walls rise almost at right angles off the road. Some trees had rounded tops sculpted by the wind; pine and oak grow on the lower steps and some near the beautiful Hodder had exposed roots showing the sandy soil, the colour of the indigenous stone. Pheasants still strutted, the fields and verges were covered with foxgloves in an almost secret world, yet another to return to when time permits.

The road from Newton to Whitewell is luxurious with the Trough beyond, an almost surreal landscape. I wallowed in this; it was motoring, the kind of motoring that deserved one of those open tourers I had seen in Waddington, through what is probably the last ancient forest of England.

To this parcel of treasures I would add Bolton-by-Bowland, at the south easterly tip of the Trough, which I approached along an avenue of lime and chestnut trees, bounded on the west by the larger of two greens, the school green. Not only did I pause en route to Waddington to find a private tour taking place in the church, but also an Aladdin's cave of an antique shop. The industrious owner Marian Howard, opens up for anyone who rings, so you can browse through the brocante after hours. I joined the tail-end church tour of a Lancashire ladies' party from Rawtenstall, who were having an evening of culture and bonhomie.

Bolton-by-Bowland was surveyed in the Domesday Book – its earlier name, Bodleton, reflects its Saxon origins. Edward III granted a charter for the market held on the smaller green which has the stocks. Bolton is worthy of Whitaker's praise; he would be delighted that still 'no manufactories' have disfigured the scene. There is no doubt that Bolton was important; silver was discovered in the sixteenth century and the family whose memorial will for ever be remembered, the Pudseys, were probably Norman. The church, on rising ground, has a stained-glass east window by Hardman, the tower is crenellated, with four pinnacles, giving, as Whitaker describes, a more elaborate air than the other churches in the area. The fortified door is studded with nails and has a large wooden peg or bolt.

The monument to the Pudsey family is without equal: a huge 10ft by 5ft limestone, structure raised above ground for protection and depicting Sir Ralph Pudsey, his two wives and twenty five children. The male children are clothed according to their profession, in either military or ecclesiastical habits. The wives are well-wimpled, the Gothic decoration is elegant and Sir Ralph's footwear is beautifully detailed. It would be fascinating to discover more about this extraordinary family and its monument for Sir Ralph's name is only presumed, not mentioned, yet his wives are.

Sir Ralph also sheltered Henry VI, at Bolton Hall after the Battle of Hexham. Whitaker's piece on Bolton in his history of Craven has illustrations of Henry's spoon, glove and boot. I agree with him, this visit 'would amply reward a traveller of taste for the trouble of a short deviation'. It is probably the most complete village in the Trough, with a post office, village shop and tea room combined, run by a lady, born here, and who I found made parkin not with oats but flour which her customers prefer. She told us, myself and one other regular tea drinker and eater, a young man of fourteen, that she was the daughter of a Yorkshire miner and granddaughter of a Lancashire farmer. She had, I was pleased to hear, read Whitaker, and told us about her father, a miner who had gone down the mines at the age of twelve and was proud to have had his first job as gate opener for the pit ponies who pulled the carts of coal.

In his book of 1950 on Lancashire Walter Greenwood has a chapter on Lancashire women. I have to use poetic licence because Waddington and Bolton were once in Yorkshire, but I must write as I find today, and have found the qualities he described among the women I met here. His ideal was no waste and a good table, never throwing anything away – pegged rugs were a testament to this. Such enterprising women live here, they are light-hearted and have a no-nonsense approach to life, whatever their age. The lady running the village shop and tea room, the owner of the antiques shop and the hotel-keeper Daphne Forbes epitomise the staying power of this happy breed. Opening for a special tour, serving tea to the end of one very rainy Sunday afternoon, and the good table at Waddington is surely the Lancashire 'way', just as it was at Gawthorpe, which was always in Lancashire. Greenwood's ideal would as 'soon put poison on the table for the family as a loaf of bread bought from a shop'.

NORTHUMBRIA

Durham Cathedral and the city of Durham

Durham

Durham is a seat in several senses: of religion, learning and justice. Firstly it is the shrine and resting place of St Cuthbert, one of the important founders of the Christian faith in England. This was also the seat of bishops who had secular as well as ecclesiastical authority. Durham is the third oldest university foundation in the England.

And lastly, Durham was a powerhouse of William the Conqueror's invasion. His castle is a stone metaphor of conquest and a bastion of strength against any would-be invader.

The train sets you down in the front stalls of the city with the cathedral as the stage almost outside the carriage. The rebuilding of the Saxon Durham Cathedral was begun in 1093 and completed by 1133, a comparatively short period and therefore a building of its own time. The city's unusual distinction is that the son of William the Conqueror developed the ingenious idea of bringing together the power of the church and the throne. He created a palatinate or secular province over which the bishops presided; a separate estate born out of the tradition of the ancient kings of Northumbria. Until the mid-seventeenth century the Bishops of Durham could raise troops and in the Middle Ages could grant licences to crenellate castles. They were great landowners. (Pre-Reformation accounts showed that the see was exceedingly rich.) Until the Reformation and dissolution of Durham's monastery in 1538-39 the bishopric was effectively independent. It was only in the 1670s that Durham achieved any representation in the Westminster parliament.

The site of this magnificent cathedral and castle could not have been better. Durham, once Dunholme, lies on a peninsula, surrounded by hills. The castle and cathedral towers face each other on the hill with the steep valley of the River Wear falling away below. One of the best views is the reflection in the water from Elvet Bridge, the castle on one side with the west end of the cathedral on the other. The church was founded in 995, (although nearby Chester-le-Street predates it by 113 years) and contains the shrines of St Cuthbert, the hermit Bishop of Lindisfarne, and the Venerable Bede. From 1000 years ago to the present day pilgrims have come to Durham.

The houses on Palace Green provide the wings of the cathedral which lies in a town close surrounded by a mixture of eighteenth-century and medieval buildings. Cosin's Hall, with its delightful shell porch and the university buildings and famous library, which can be seen with permission, are now sandwiched with those belonging to the church. Much of the cathedral carving is Romanesque; it is the pillars which one never forgets, superb in their outstanding girth and design. These carvings are incised as much as five inches thick on the columns. Some are cut with a chevron pattern, or fluted or cross check designs. The remaining textures and materials are legion: a heavily carved fifteenth-century stall and Frosterly marble to enhance the piers. In the south aisle there is a painted stone seat, a sedilla near the chantry tomb, and the bishops' throne is bright, ornate and painted. The ribs of the crossing have Romanesque cuttings, while the sixteenth-century painted clock case reminds one of just how much was lost to vandalism; the whole cathedral was once full of colour.

There is a list of the bishops from 995 to 1994 on one side, and priors on the other from 1084 to 1540, the year that Hugh Whitehead changed his title from prior to dean. The names of the deans run from 1541 to 1989. Thomas Wolseley was a bishop from 1523 to 1529, Neville in 1257, Walter Skirlaw from 1388 to 1406, of whom more at Howden (see page 115), Robert of Holy Island from 1274 to 1283, and Philip de Poitou from 1197 to 1208. These names resonate with the very history of England.

I have not seen anything to compare with the carved porch and door leading from the cloisters, where it was customary to let children play on Shrove Tuesday, to the main body of the church. An ogee-headed doorway leads to a wonderful cloister with a fifteenth-century wooden ceiling. But it is the twelfth-century door that I remember best. This is studded, with intricate scrollwork and banding strong enough to keep anyone out, built by Bishop Geoffry Rufus between 1133 and 1140. Late one winter evening as I left the cloister a spotlight on the opposite side of the garth showed up the shape of the carving and reflected in son et lumière fashion on to the solid wall behind where I stood, so that the carving in shades of grey-brown and black produced extraordinary three-dimensional images from the reflected monks' dormitory windows. Late afternoon in winter is the time to visit this wonderful church, open until the close of Evensong. There can be no other cathedral that has this massive strength.

Sir Timothy Eden called Durham a civilised city, and I had the most spectacular view of the cathedral as I travelled down South Street, a cobbled winding lane with a good range of houses on the left from all periods and trees on the side facing the river below. In the late eighteenth century a Pole, Joseph Boruwlaski, who settled here and was buried in the cathedral, wrote in his memoirs in 1820 of the polite society he found here. Doubtless he was entertained in these Georgian houses. One of his particular friends was Stephen Kemble, brother of Charles who was the theatre manager and whose sister Fanny Kemble performed here. This acting family made their own dresses, pies and puddings and patched and darned in the morning, before donning their patches and rouge in the evening.

Durham is steep and for the fit – all students must be so – and there are steeply rising lanes up to the castle and university after you cross the bridge. From Silver Street I took Moatside Lane, the medieval pilgrims' route to the Cathedral, and left into an alleyway, quite secret, with the castle wall on my right. I eventually reached the castle mound. Here are medieval houses and wonderful shop fronts. A former robe maker and tailor has wood carving and curved windows. Leading off the vennell (lanes) Drury Lane's steps drop from the alleyways back down to the river. Number 43 appears to have three doors and along another alleyway one finds the site of the original North Gate, between the Bailey and the city, rebuilt in 1420 in what seems to be the middle of a house.

North Bailey has elegant Georgian town houses curving into Owengate, housing mostly students, where music, and not all pop, mingled with voices, bursts out from open windows. Outside the close the houses are set into the hill with first-floor balconies to make the most of the views. Crossgate is one of the steepest streets, leading up from Framwellgate Bridge past St Margaret's Church, the Angel Inn and the Old Elm Tree pub, past Grape Lane and up along the path to Neville's Cross. In each quarter the medieval streets, alleyways and Georgian terraces add to the fascinating townscape and in Durham style the allotments of St Margaret's have an almost grand surrounding hawthorn hedge.

Returning later to the Almshouses café and restaurant in the Palace Green in Bishop John Cosin's seventeenth-century almshouses, I was not let down. Although it was the end of the day they managed a salad of crisp leaves, tomato and lamb's lettuce. A wide counter in steel and glass had large platters still bearing fruit, cakes and pies; the salad they managed to prepare proved to be a high tea. Virtually all the cakes made here are on view and different coffees are on offer in this inviting spot where students and lecturers hang in with the humble tourist. And as extras we had the cast of a Puccini-performing travelling opera who were refuelling themselves before their journey south.

The dishes one might find are fennel and potato soup, broccoli and stilton quiches (should it be flan up here?) and Cumberland sausage, with interesting sounding mixtures such as aubergine, tomato and toasted cashew nuts, and butter bean coriander pate (I used to make a similar dish to this in my own tea house) and some unusual sandwich fillings. Together with the cakes, there is treacle tart and bread and butter pudding. Once served you take your food through into a double-height room with stone mullions, without music, hung with pictures on sturdy paper clips, painted at the higher level in a shade of grape with modern furniture of 1950s Swedish derivation.

They persuaded me to try a piece of the lemon-flavoured passion cake for which I have to confess I do not normally have a passion; this was good, not cloyingly sweet as the shop variety often is. I would have tried all the cakes, they looked so tempting, if I had time for another round of the city. I congratulate the staff whose attitude is spot-on; they know how to welcome travellers. On another visit we wanted to take some food on the train and they kindly sliced a chunk of farmhouse cheese and bread and a piece of their caramel walnut cake which gave our plastic cup of British Rail tea another dimension.

16

Low Urpeth Farm, Chester-le-Street

Co Durham

I regret that I do not find myself at Low Urpeth often enough, but if I am working in the area I really make an effort to reserve a room. This must be one of the very few farms left in the area between Newcastle and the Pennines, really the heart of what was once the Durham minefields. Although I can see a great wave of lights of the distant metropolis, ever sprawling, so it seems, this place is both peaceful and exceptionally cosy in winter after a good walk around hilltop Durham.

Hilary Johnson surpasses many others with her good cheer. I want for nothing from the moment I cross the threshold through the farmyard, arriving weary from the long journey north. Low Urpeth Farm is a solid, generous Victorian square house which has a good view of farmland from the breakfast room with its comfortable mahogany furniture and a good helping of its original features: the ceiling roses and good skirtings, carved cornices in the dining room, and a pleasant staircase with unusual shallow treads.

Low Urpeth has arable crops but principally farms trees specially for nature conservation: indigenous oak and ash. The friendly labrador and the cat which decided that the roof of my car was a good watching place give the farmyard feel. From the comforting tray of tea served in the relaxing sitting room to the well-thought-out bedrooms, there is nothing to fault. For Hilary truly understands a traveller's needs: to relax and unwind; this is the reason why so many of her guests stay regularly. There are beautiful little touches, proper chairs in the room, ample space to move and spread out papers and books, and very large enveloping towels (why is there a generally a meanness with towels?). The lighting is good, imperative for me as I am often working, and the breakfast lives up to expectations.

A vast Victorian buffet with back mirrors and ornate carved handles is laden with bowls of fresh fruit salad, dried fruit and every imaginable cereal. Shutters at the windows make it even cosier. It was here that I first tried the Loughbrow jams that are now sold at Washington (see page 85). But Hilary uses as much local produce as possible, and recently I sampled marmalade from Broxbushes at Corbridge filled with robust chunks of peel and a tart taste. In addition there is a choice of lemon cheese and local honeycomb to spread on your toast. One sits at the large oak table on substantial leather-seated chairs with whoever else is staying, which I much prefer to the lonely, guest house style of single tables. This is comfort with a large C, and Hilary's fresh white apron symbolises her professional approach to the business of providing for her guests.

I also enjoy staying at Low Urpeth in the summer when I have been lucky enough to find one or two locals to gossip with over the allotment walls. Here you should find some of the greatest leek growers in the world, where about hundred years ago for Saturday tea both the green and white part of the leeks were fried in the fat of good bacon and then served up with the bacon, bread and a pot of tea. I am a leek fanatic and can eat them in every which way I can conceive, even amalgamating a December picking with scrambled free-range eggs. Pull, eat fresh and crisp and do not spoil with water! Traditionally the small mining villages had good allotments often sited opposite their terraced

houses; the plots have low surrounding walls and are enriched by their marvellous organic sheds and pigeon coops. The powers that be have realised their worth, and some of them are being listed because they are indeed part of the landscape and regional culture.

17

Alnwick and Hipsburn

Northumberland

From Alnmouth, a small seaside village, so near Newcastle and yet so far, a soft sort of place that looks out to a bay across restful golden sands, I discovered more of Northumberland. I had travelled from Washington, through Morpeth with an interesting town hall, delightful red brick Georgian houses, an excellent and nationally famous cheese emporium and the thirteenth-century Chantry. Morpeth is yet another town to dally in and perhaps make your own architectural trail.

The farmhouse at Hipsburn, managed by Mr and Mrs Tulip, was a good location for this northern sojourn, between coast and hills and perfect for walking. Unlike the road to Jedburgh and Carter Bar, the road north to Alnwick is far from rugged and the roads are bordered with honeysuckle mingling with hawthorn. The verdant wide valleys are appealing even in the fine misty rain days of early June. The Aln and Amble rivers feed and fertilise this corn-growing country, and the rain makes rich pasture for the black cattle.

Beatrix Potter described Alnwick as a 'fine old-fashioned place with cobbled streets'. She travelled through with her parents in 1894 and liked the area between here and the Cheviots: 'the stations remarkably good, and here they cultivate tomato plants in their waiting rooms'. What a good idea; do they still do it I wonder? Alnwick is still a fine town where folk going into market dress accordingly. I hope it continues, along with the market square focus; plans are being mooted to pedestrianise the cobbled area, which must maintain the essence of the town, for market places are the last open-air locations for socialising and informal communal activities, an essential part of our social and architectural heritage. Plans, on the other hand, to build a second supermarket on the outskirts have been scuppered. Alnwick has an impressive market hall and the Northumberland Hall, where I took time to sit and sign against the planned supermarket encroachment and where I understand they hold coffee mornings. I am sure that William Cobbett, nineteenth-century traveller and reporter of England who was scathing of large businesses – his 'stock jobbers' – would have done the same.

The approach to the castle over the bridge by Robert Adam with its powerful Percy signature, a lion cast in lead, standing astride the embattled parapet, is preferred. The castle is enhanced by landscaped parkland designed by Capability Brown (born at Cambo near Wallington Hall which has some of the most enchanting walled gardens in the North). Here is another instance of medieval men making the most of hill and aspect. Alnwick's situation is gentler, contrasting with its neighbours at Dunstanburgh and Warkworth, yet castle and town meld well on this eastern approach. Pevsner considered the barbican added by the second Henry de Percy in the castle's hey day 'the best in the country'. Beatrix Potter, however, found it 'black dark with odd statues on the battlements in quaint threatening attitudes'. The castle interior is far from threatening, if anything too much restored by Anthony Salvin for me, with little evidence of Adam's work; but the lofty double-height library is a gilded and striking space large enough to lose oneself in. And in the grounds there is a splendid ornate example of Adam's Gothicising design at the Brizzell tower which is seventy-eight feet high; folly not fortification and reflecting the first Duke of Northumberland's love of the Picturesque.

But I was hunting out the contemporary craft work of Mr Tulip, a local farmer, craftsman and stick carver, having heard earlier in the day from his son and grandson that this could be seen in the castle. I saw the fruits of his labours proudly displayed. As many as thirty five are on show. Norman Tulip carves the heads of sheep, mice, herons, peacocks, snakes and fish out of ram's horn with shanks made of blackthorn and fruit woods such as plum or holly. The horn is fixed to the shank by pins and different-coloured writing inks are used to add a true-to-life element to the ornate carvings. Animals are used as references and the sticks go through a very long process of whittling, carving and sanding over more than seventy hours for a simple crook or as many as 400 for a lobster that I am sure even Dali would have enjoyed. That very week the local paper reported a move to ban the use of horn; how sad it would be to lose another agricultural craft.

My search for northern taste was well rewarded at Mrs Tulip's house. Her farmhouse is caring and comfortable. It was built in about 1850, although some remains indicate a thirteenth-century settlement which would tie in comfortably with the building of the Warkworth and Alnwick. It is a spacious house with views of either a large vegetable garden or the sea and is not over-furnished. Everything has been considered, even the welcoming piece of homemade fruit cake on my tray at teatime but the sharp and tempting smell of homemade lemon curd which greeted me one evening as it bubbled on the Aga – deep yellow, glossy, soothing and served fresh for breakfast the next day – was the best treat could you expect after a day feckling about in the fine mist. Mrs Tulip serves local eggs and of course kippers from Craster, enjoyed with company at one large table.

One of my fellow guests here at Hipsburn was a retired miner who loves this coast. There are no working pits here now, and

there is no vestige of that enveloping coat of black dust from which everyone wanted to escape. But there are first hand stories to be gained from speaking to the miners who lived and worked the pits until quite recently, and there are plenty to tell the tale. I found A J Cronin's The Stars Look Down an atmospheric and profoundly down-to-earth story of the dark enveloping horror of the pits. Nearly every miner or his family was left with a legacy no one else would want to inherit. There was no respite from abject poverty, not even a chance of a herring, or a 'bit left-ower' from the butchers for tea; this contrasted with their rare trip taken to Whitley Bay and Cullercoats, surely as wonderful for them as a present day first encounter with the Mediterranean, well, perhaps thirty years ago. Cronin's hero and friends ate 'unbelievably of ice cream and fruit' and visited queer crab parlours sitting on horse-hair sofas to eat the fresh crab meat out of the shell. Really fresh meaty crab in a sandwich or salad at a seaside café is still a delightful treat.

18

Chesters

Northumberland

Walking along the Roman wall is one of the most exciting pastimes imaginable in this country. The sheer size, the concept, the completion, the dogged, relentless mastery over climate and country by Hadrian are incomprehensible, yet here it is.

The Romans took their wall up and over every hill they encountered using the rocks they found rather than starting afresh. From mile castle to numbered mile castle, this can be traced and followed to the point where the wall meets the Great Whin Sill with high drama. The purpose was administrative as well as defensive. A mile castle or perhaps a minor fort housed thirty-two men with six in a turret who patrolled twenty-four hours a day, but the local farmers and traders were granted access. The remains help to piece together the story of the wall which travels sometimes at right angles to the ground.

There is a weighty choice of centres interpreting the forts that have been excavated. Housesteads and Vindolanda could take two or three days. I settled for Chesters because it had the original museum for John Clayton's collection designed by Norman Shaw in the late 1890s with its vigorous eaves, so appropriate for this climate, and a favourite small museum. (Sir Norman Shaw also designed Cragside for Lord Armstrong.) I suspect this dates me, but I prefer museums with collections that speak for themselves. I also wanted to see the new centre that the Napper Collerton partnership had designed at Corbridge in the 1980s. This is of an unassuming, modern and not intrusive character, sitting side-on to the site. The clerestory, verandah and combination of wood and slate is cool and crisp in design but also successful in its clever use of the right materials. This makes an interesting comparison with Shaw's museum.

Chesters is located in a wonderful parkland setting; the museum embodies its time and Shaw's small classical building, set near the stables also designed by him, is unconspicuous, with a fitness for its purpose. The cabinets and displays are original; the whole roof space and walls are used effectively. And this builds on the tradition of the house nearby (incidentally designed by John Carr) for John Clayton the archaeologist an associate of the architects Grainger and Dobson who made their mark in eighteenth-century Newcastle.

The Chesters fort is built on a hill, as part of the wall, with excellent views over the Tyne at the lower level. The bath house located close to the swift-flowing river is a temple to cleanliness, and as I walked around I could relate the various hot rooms with what happens today in health spas. This was designed 2000 years ago. The first room is the changing room with stone niches, not unlike the seats in a medieval chapter house. After this the Roman officers could choose from the different rooms with their different mechanisms: cold bath, sauna and steam heat of varying degrees, and one specifically for scrubbing and scraping the dirt away, an apsidal room, followed by the equivalent of a plunge pool to close the pores. The baths are vaulted and even the ribs of the voussoirs or openings are designed with an early ventilation technique with flues to take the steam away, and the tiled remains in the apse are from a type of damp proofing.

The stoke house or boiler conducts the heat so that it is cleverly circulated above and below. The walls of each room are thick and lichen grows at the base of the columns. Nearby the yews soften and complement this exceptional setting for a bath house, sheltered by the incline and heated up by the sun. It was important that all the troops had their weekly bath, the bath house was not just a luxury for officers. The hypercaust (heat conduit) and the vallum or ditch can still be seen, and as the barracks would have taken the full force of the north winds the commanding officer's house lies in more sheltered position further down the hill, where the hypercaust would reduce the effect of the elements with under-floor heating. The situation, aspect and materials – great fat stone slabs – are a wonder of the site and many other forts follow the same principle: the praetorium or big house for the commander, barracks for the foot, and depending on the importance of each fort, a headquarters building for the civilian settlement. Chesters has all these and four gateways which an artist's impression illustrates, as well as the elegance employed in the very functional quarters with their Tuscan

columns. The barrack room was barracklike, and everything is set out in straight lines with accommodation in ranks, normally sleeping ten but here eight each side.

At Chesters food for visitors is all homemade and sells out quickly. I was not able to taste but through one of those perfect coincidences which often accompany my travels I met a very old friend and her husband whom I had not seen for more than ten years, who had taken the soup and tasted the homemade scone which were given a thumbs up. The tea room was full of shelves of homemade jams to take away.

Today people can take their holiday and walk beside the fortifications for pleasure and relate to these conquerors and civilisers with regard to food and hygiene. For the Romans brought vines and grew grapes, they had food from home; 'a friend sent me fifty oysters from Cordonivi' was one of the commonplace comments found on the Vindolanda tablets. Garlic, olives, olive oil, all those Mediterranean ingredients were listed in the accounts and are archaeological proof of what many believe to be newly invented fashions.

19

Chillingham Castle

Northumberland

When I saw the sign telling me that Berwick was thirteen miles further north I realised just how near the borders I was, and Chillingham is part of the border history. This castle was built determinedly for defence, and the recent restoration of Chillingham is unquestionably being forged with equal resolution. Chillingham Castle is situated in unspoiled, rolling landscape, among a pleasant patchwork of arable land and trees conserved because the estates have remained intact.

From Chillingham this landscape leads to the foot-hills of the Cheviots. Chillingham, for many, recalls the famous white cattle recorded so graphically in Thomas Bewick's wood blocks, but these wonderful beasts inspired others including Landseer. The cattle or the wild ox (Bos taurus) graze and roam free now as they have done since the twelfth century. They have miraculously survived disease and horrendous winters, indeed they may have been enclosed here since the Roman occupation. Although visitors pay to see them, the animals are not always on view. This part of the visit is just like any other nature reserve; a ranger accompanies and visitors need to bring binoculars to catch sight of the herd if it is in the hills.

You approach the ancient sandstone castle along a lime-bounded drive, with a high crenellated wall on the right which makes a fitting introduction to an unusual visit. Chillingham was almost a ruin when acquired by Sir Humphrey Wakefield, whose wife is a direct descendent of the Grey family. The castle, originally fortified in the twelfth century, stands four-square with a formal entrance into the courtyard. Immediately, you are safely surrounded on all sides. A further set of steps on the opposite south end leads to the museum and state rooms. The original tower captured by the Grey family was extended and granted a licence to crenellate and fortify in 1344. The castle lived and played its part in both national and border troubles to the hilt, was constantly attacked and housed as many as a hundred horsemen within its fortified walls. King Henry II famously stayed here, as did Edward I, Hammer of the Scots, as he planned his northern forays. It suffered further onslaught during the rebellion of 1536, which had repercussions all over the North. In this county local families fought one another, and the Percys of nearby Alnwick led the 1536 assault here.

Neither did Chillingham entirely escape the vagaries of architectural fashions and rebuilding. The long galleries were a sixteenth-century innovation, the eighteenth century brought some changes to the fenestration and even the quadrangle acquired another flight of steps as the castle took on a completely new mantle, requiring more servants to service the larger numbers of guests. A complete but hidden new kitchen wing was added in 1791 by the Edinburgh architect John Paterson. Sir Jeffry Wyatville, then at the peak of his royal success at Windsor, was called in 1828, and the castle changed from a stronghold to a house of leisure. Wyatville even imported pieces to delight the eye such as a magnificent pair of marble fireplaces designed by Colen Campbell for the then recently demolished Wanstead in Essex. Wyatville added avenues and lodges, planting out the lawns which had been built up over the moat in 1732. Subsequently the village itself was added by the architect Sir Edward Blore.

Chillingham is an undiscovered kind of place, unlike nearby Bamburgh Castle, which has another marvellous setting on the cliffs rising above the palest, soft fudge-coloured beach. Bamburgh is ordered and restored in the last century whereas at Chillingham one felt there were still old layers behind the changes yet to be peeled away and recorded. New finds and documents show that the Grey family's standard was seen at many famous battles, such as Crecy and Agincourt, and at Henry VIII's Field of the Cloth of Gold. And true to tradition there are ghosts. All the surfaces are worn with love and years of use, not over polished; there are great chunks of stone resting against walls, and mill wheels against windows. The ongoing restoration raises questions: what period does one restore and which generation's craftsmanship does one lay bare? Should the decay of each generation be covered up, and who are we to choose? The present owner Sir Humphrey Wakefield asks these questions. This is not a precise guidebook visit where everything is in its place, rather an excursion into delightful dilapidation with a post-modernist approach to historic house presentation.

The painted buffets, the chairs with broken backs, the animated guides and the lady who sits making her rag rugs mark today's enthusiasm for the past. Amusing signs and collections of boots sit on the stairs. There are piles of magazines and everywhere you are aware of the odds and ends of living which even castle owners' families generate. This unusual approach attracts young children who can touch without being told not to, and lift to their heart's delight even the lid of the wooden latrine in the tower.

The bedrooms are friendly; travelling cases are stacked up, and the rugs are well worn. The James I drawing room has a wonderful set of high-backed caned William and Mary chairs and is set out for a game of cards. Here the plasterwork of 1600 has a three-dimensional pendent design which only just survived well enough to be restored. The silk wallpaper, originally a 1760 pattern for Chatsworth, was run off from the original blocks and woven for Chillingham. It should not be forgotten that this house was unoccupied for more than fifty years. The Army used the castle in the Second World War, burning down the north wing and keeping warm with fires fuelled with Elizabethan oak panelling.

The woodland walk and an elegant avenue of beautiful mature trees lead to a distant focal point with an equestrian statue. Sheep graze between the lush trees in an untouched medieval landscape. If you cannot visit the castle during the season you can actually stay, making a choice from a selection of accommodation: the nineteenth-century wing in rooms hung with Sir Edwin Landseer's paintings, a dairy, or the coaching rooms, or in a separate eighteenth-century house. From time to time local antique auctions are held here. As a day visitor or when staying longer the pleasures of the landscape, parkland and nearby estate village are there to be enjoyed, and of course the peace of the border country is free.

The tea room is modest but nonetheless friendly and the baking is done in the best tradition by local ladies; it is small enough for visitors who have come to this spot in the middle of nowhere to feel relaxed enough to converse and exchange enthusiasms. The prices are affordable and there are about eleven different cakes, including sponges, lemon cakes and gingerbread, as well as shortbread with two varieties of scones, on offer. These are set out simply on a small checked cloth. Flans and homemade soup are available for those who want something more filling. Who needs sophistication in such a situation?

20

Craster and Dunstanburgh Castle

Northumberland

What do you write when you find an indescribable location, leave it to J M W Turner? Or emulate Coleridge who, when he came upon something he himself could not describe, wrote 'no words could convey any idea of this prestigious wilderness'. Turner did it best with his view of the extraordinary Dunstanburgh Castle, from the south with a wild sea in the foreground which he painted at dawn, possibly leaving Craster at night to reach his favoured spot; his picture now hangs in Newcastle.

I was captivated and spent several hours over two days on this excursion which centred on castles, kippers and a marvellous coastline. As you travel through the fields from Alnwick, the terrain is not unlike the roads that lead to the Norfolk coast, winding, with walks begging to be taken. A double arch or gateway that belongs to Craster Tower leads to the village, with subtle glimpses of stone creating the setting.

Craster village and its small harbour, where the fishing industry has taken place since the seventeenth century, recall the once-thriving local industry – herring. Kippers were a north-eastern innovation. The quantity landed in the early part of the twentieth century was enough to give work to hundreds of women. Now only a row of cottages, a small public garden above the detritus of lobster and crab pots and the harbour built in 1906 are all that remain. The pride of place today goes to the Robson Smokery, which also sells salmon pâté, kippers galore and fat brown crabs. Once tasted, these kippers can be addictive. Robsons, fortunately can satisfy all fishy cravings with their postal service. The herrings are gutted, soaked in brine, hung on hooks and then smoked to give their succulent fulsome flavour.

The village could double as a film set, but the smokery of Robsons is real enough: black, charred, wooden-walled, and also in danger of losing the special aromatic qualities that the oakwood panelled smokery and chips supply to the smoking, because of legislation. I was shown the processes which take place behind the long stone wall with red pantiles that faces the sea.

Local fishermen still take out their small cobles, catching crab and lobster in the winter, salmon and sea trout in the summer. From Craster one can also walk further up the coast to Low Newton around Embleton and then take the coast road to Bamburgh. I liked the nineteenth century village where the main street runs neatly with estate houses down to the castle. The coast road is empty; it follows the seashore and sand. Embleton Church is worth seeing for the unusual tower which has an open parapet, small trefoil panels and pinnacles decorated and carved quite unlike the tower of St Lawrence at Warkworth.

But the mile or so from Craster harbour to Dunstanburgh has to be made whatever the weather. As you leave the village you cross the fields where Limousin cattle lounge, to the ruins that rise up ahead. At first, small as you approach they begin to mesmerise as the remains of the castle pierce the sky like two large stone tulip-shaped tentacles. They are dramatic, and as I walked up the southern slope on the morning of Midsummer's Day I thought about the suitability of this position for a performance of that Scottish play, what a marvellous stage.

This natural site has been a point of defence since Iron Age man settled here, through the Roman occupation, and of course its worst moments in the fourteenth century. This dominating castle was strengthened by John of Gaunt while he defended the Scottish marches in 1380. What is left has not been altered since it was built in the early fourteenth century; the striking differences between this and other nearby castles is that the sea has provided a completely natural north wall, where the sheer drop below was and is impenetrable. Originally there were three storeys, then a further two of flat semicircular towers were added to strengthen the southern approach, the easiest to assail. The living quarters were located here along with the main defence. It has been in ruins since the sixteenth century, having been won and lost several times during the Wars of the Roses. Anyone who sees these extraordinary ruins will not forget their impact.

21

Hexham Abbey, Hexham and Blanchland

Northumberland

Every route to Hexham from the south-west, through the Pennines and Alston, or from Barnard Castle, is attractive. William Cobbett remarked that the 'county seems to be wholly destitute of people'. It is still uncrowded. He also described the avenue of trees which still flourishes. Hexham lies between Carlisle and Newcastle; it is truly a centre, an old and venerable place, yet surprisingly, though almost on top of the Roman wall, not colonised by them. This is riding, hacking and eventing terrain. I was delighted to discover that Celia Fiennes rode here in 1698. Today another green, pristine green, sport of bowls is played behind the abbey.

Hexham has a generosity of spirit, from the mature lofty plantations on the approach roads to the cries of the witty market traders, the time-to-talk shopkeepers, the heartfelt greeting by the abbey guides and to their simple little refreshment room, where butter is spread charitably. The South and North Tyne rivers meet below Hexham, which lies on a bluff. The town is close set around the abbey with a moot hall and a small, colourful, congenial market with a wood shambles embellished with Tuscan columns, the focal point for a town visit, especially on Tuesdays. The moot hall, however, has a more forbidding and dominating presence for it was used to house the court until 1838 and follows a similar form to a castle gate house. Here the gatehouse is more of a fourteenth-century civic centre or stronghold built in sandstone and limestone.

On the domestic front Hexham still has its individual small shop fronts, and several can be found right opposite the abbey, one a fishmonger, one of two in the town which sells Arbroath smokies and fresh herrings from a tiled interior. From the abbey the cloisters lead to the park with the charming bandstand, donated in 1912 by Henry Bell and curving seats surrounded by flowers for watching the bowls, make a softer contrast to the town side.

Hexham has a similar history of separateness to Durham. In

about 674 Queen Aethelfryth, married to the King of Northumbria, gave the land to Wilfrid, Bishop of York. Thus the regality of Hexham or ecclesiastical kingdom was ruled in isolation with its own laws until it was sacked by the Danes in 875. The way in to the abbey is right on the square through an enclosed stone entrance called the Slype; there is no separating close as the medieval houses have been destroyed.

The stones of Hexham Abbey tell many tales. The Romans may not have settled just here but stones from Corbridge were used to build the most exceptional feature of the church, the seventh-century Saxon crypt, celebrating the life of Wilfrid who dedicated the church to St Andrew the patron saint of the abbey. Here, above all, there is an intimate connection with the pilgrims who went down these stairs more than 1300 years ago to see the reliquary where niches held the oil-burning lamps. It is a time trip that is immediate because of its size. The engravings and graffiti are Roman, celebrating the prowess of a centurion; a remarkable, historical, sacred and architectural treasure which remained hidden until the eighteenth century. Moreover, the stones of the night stair in the wall of the south transept make a dramatic flight of steps down which the Augustinian order descended to worship and still act as a processional route for the choir. The colossal stone crossing tower with its magnificent springing is the best place to stand and digest the abbey, significantly rising high, probably the highest in the county. But the most important stone artefact is the stone or tub chair called the Frith stool, carved in one massive piece with an incised decorative motif which gives credence to the bishop's importance and role.

There are remains of some carved misericords, no canopies alas, yet some nutmeg-shaped decoration on the hood moulds of the chancel. The nave was rebuilt by Temple Moore, that prolific Yorkshire church restorer, in 1907.

A small room off the cloister acts as a simple tea room open only in summer, so I advise catching this while you can. It is managed by volunteers who will spoil you. They made time to butter some scones and give me a piece of Northrumbrian tea bread for a picnic; the quality was unequalled on that particular journey. The frugal furniture has been softened with seersucker tablecloths which, with cottage garden posies, make a heartfelt welcome. Prices are amazing, with no hint of portion control. The homemade soups, tomato and carrot, leek and potato and cream of vegetable, are very popular and the cakes are the real thing, all made with the best ingredients. There are choices of lemon curd cake, which has a whole jar of curd slurped into the mixture; rich coffee cake becomes more luxurious with ground almonds and in their season I saw little dishes of local strawberries which grow well in this land of becks and rivers.

With stone and monasteries as a recurring theme, this might be a suitable place to include a pause at Blanchland. For some years people had asked if I had been here and I felt I had to see why. Blanchland lives up to its reputation, a brilliant shining village whose context was a golden copse of trees. It nestles between moor and fell where the River Derwent twinkles and twists, and where county boundaries switch repeatedly back and forth between Durham and Northumberland. If ever a village arrived by default this is the candidate.

Blanchland is all stone, some of it creeper-covered, and it is almost enclosed. At the centre is an unusual L-shaped courtyard, not a medieval village but an eighteenth-century one constructed from the stone of the monastery which is incorporated into it. The abbey was founded by the Premonstration order in the twelfth century, an offshoot of the Augustinians. Today the delightful rows of cottages and the village shop and post office located in a tower make the centre of Blanchland piazza-like, and a 'model village' incomparable in England.

Stop at the Crewe Arms, which has a charming trefoil-headed front entrance and unusual carved porch to the right of the tower. This is Georgian but was once the abbot's lodging, and here you gain some idea of the setting of the earlier buildings. The hotel, whose garden can be seen from the small room with a marvellous twelfth-century fireplace, transports you into what was once the guest house which looked on to the cloister, and the wall on the left, forms the choir of the present church. The other building which predominates the square is a crenellated tower and arch. The pleasant village stores, set in the middle of one side of the vertical run of the square, sell a mixture of food and gifts such as locally gathered flower-power honey. To round off this unusual visit I suggest a stroll behind the houses where there is a row of extremely fertile-looking kitchen gardens to a house that sells honeycomb. This means going down the kitchen passage of the house where you see the 'Honey for sale' sign.

Warkworth Castle and Warkworth village

Northumberland

It would not be an exaggeration to say that Warkworth is one of the most exciting places I have encountered in England. With the church of St Lawrence at one end of a village street rising up to the castle at the other, this is almost a text-book medieval village. To experience the finest impact you should approach from the north on the road which crosses the River Coquet; the original bridge, still in perfect order, is one of only a handful of fortified bridges in the whole country.

From the foot of Castle Street, the grandeur of the curving ascent to the castle at the top can be really be admired. I arrived in a June downpour and was amused to read that J M W Turner, who made his tour de force visit to the North in 1797, arrived and painted Warkworth Castle against a thunderstorm.

The elegant sandstone church of St Lawrence, which pre-dates the castle, has the largest nave in Northumberland. It was used as a refuge during border fighting and lies in the lower loop of the river, with cool copper beech trees in a nigh-perfect setting. The nave wall has some unusual robust buttresses, flat with the wall, very simple round arched windows, extremely delicate lancet windows in the tower, a small, almost complete, Norman church. This was the scene of the proclamation of the Old Pretender in 1715, and here the rebellious Scots tried to force the then incumbent to pray for James III of Scotland, without success. Only fifty six years later John Wesley, the preacher of such stamina whose path I seemed to cross repeatedly in my own Northern excursions, also preached here.

St Lawrence's was frequently attacked after its construction in 787, burnt by the Scots in 1174 then rebuilt by the Normans as a church and stronghold. Although the church was restored by the Victorians every century has left its own evidence: the robust round Saxon chancel, the Norman rib vaulting (one of few examples influenced by Durham) the twelfth-century tower, the thirteenth-century vestry and the fifteenth-century aisles.

The sixteenth century is represented by Matthew White's

ironwork close or rather market square, in the foreground.

One or two houses either side of the church have interesting fanlights, mostly of nineteenth-century origin, in particular the former vicarage, now Abbeyfield House. Just over one hundred years ago Richard Watson Dixon wrote a history of the Church of England there and entertained the poets Newbolt and Bridges. At the back of the church behind the wall there is a row of cottages with picturesque porches. As you make the wonderful walk up to the castle elegant houses line the street.

Warkworth Castle was built by the Percy family after the Conquest, and just as Dunstanburgh and Bamburgh it stands on a gift of a site. The position gave its occupants far-reaching-views. Originally it had a deep ditch on the steep side falling away above the river which formed the first line of defence from the southwest. The keep is far and away the most interesting point which faces north and has eight projecting points of a square. Five of these projections stretch out towards the village.

The castle was entered through the great gate on the south over a bridge and moat. To strengthen it further a series of towers was built into the whole, surrounding four curtain walls. Inside the walls are the remains of a chapel, solar, brewhouse and kitchen. Constructed by design for self-sufficiency and self-defence, the relationship of the service spaces to the formal areas is nothing if not modern. The ground floor and first floor can be viewed, and English Heritage, which cares for the property, hopes in due course to open all the keep to visitors. Looking at the plan it appears that the functional spaces within have dictated a truly architectonic building, showing that in the late fourteenth century function and aesthetic were seamless.

Warkworth Castle illustrates the evolution of castles which also became homes with a degree of comfort while retaining the former twelfth-century formal defence plan. Inside the keep a second suite of rooms was constructed, quite self-contained – cellar, buttery, and kitchen – enabling the Percys to withhold prolonged attack. The Percy properties and estates spanned the whole country, here their stone fortress is a metaphor for that power and strength. This castle was also a pivot of northern hunting and feasting – society and defence. It became an aristocratic

fortified residence. From its humble beginnings with the usual motte and bailey it was transformed sufficiently to entertain Edward I. With some imagination it is not difficult to visualise the feasts, the tastings, the colour, and the noble lords and their courtly life. What makes the keep and the eight-pointed Greek cross shape which will have supplanted an

original square tower so exceptional and such an architectural exemplar is its combination of position and function.

The ownership switched back and forth from the Percys to the Crown and the Nevilles, but was not to regain its fifteenth-century standing and prestige after the middle of the sixteenth century when it started to fall into disrepair. The Percys, although originally a Yorkshire family, had gained such respect with the population, that they were given Warkworth by Edward III. With Alnwick, their summer home, they managed their castles so efficiently that even after defeat in the Civil War this stronghold was always given back to the family 'who have the hertes of the people of the North' in Shakespeare's Henry V.

The village thrives, as I understand from the present vicar. In the summer it holds a pageant and the village shop is a cornerstone for locals and visitors. Most of the commodities one would need are here, from postcards to bacon. It will do you proud if you need to buy for a picnic, perhaps a late one by the river (it opens until 9pm), or to take home. Much of the food is locally produced. The bread is baked in Amble, the kippers come from Craster, there is local cheese, organic mustard and jams from Berwick-upon-Tweed, as well as locally gathered honey. I can vouch for the excellent organic plum cake. The Mason's Arms next door, where the Jacobite rebels dined and where their names are carved on one of the beams, also support local fishermen. The cod that you are given here is so fresh that it does not need to see the inside of a freezer.

23

Wildfowl and Wetlands, and Washington Old Hall, Washington

Tyne and Wear

Between the A1 at Durham, and excursions into Northumberland, you will pass Washington, a new town, yet with its own history. This area grew from its natural resources; iron ore was nearby as well as coal, turning farm land into the engine of the Industrial Revolution with facilities to export and distribute at the coast. For almost 300 hundred years Durham has been producing the fuel for the shipping and glass industries in Sunderland. Thousands of trees were lost as the population grew and domestic fuel was also needed. The coal seam ran through and the first steam engine was run here at Oxclose in 1718 to pump the coal mine.

Coal was the business and the bedrock. In 1787 two million tons were shipped out from the rivers Tyne and Wear, and many lives were lost in the mining process. But today the Big Pit is a museum and there is little other than rows of cottages and allotments to revoke the colliery villages. John Wesley came here 1745 and continued to preach in County Durham until the year before he died in 1791; giving workers hope in troubled times, and coinciding with the enormous growth of industry.

The name of Washington is possibly an anglicised derivation from the Norman family of de Wessyngtons who came here in the twelfth century. It has also given its name to one of the most famous men in the world, George Washington, the first president of the United States. His forebears lived in Washington Old Hall until 1613 when they sold the house and his grandfather emigrated to America in 1656. This early Norman manor house was no more than a tenement by the 1930s but was fortunately rescued through Anglo-American initiatives and restored in 1955. The seventeenth-century house, which belongs to the National Trust, and the village is in the middle of the new town, which is divided into numbered districts. The house is spacious, warm, wide with wooden stairs, some delightful Jacobean panelling and, of course, a whole room of George Washington memorabilia.

From this combination a new green town was developed in the 1970s and what might seem unusual, the Wildfowl and Wetlands Centre at Washington was built in 1975 by Sir Peter Scott, the renowned conservationist, on land given by the Washington Development Corporation under the then leader James Steel, later knighted. The park which today abuts the 103 acres of the centre is named afetr him. Sir James was a keen bird-watcher and invited Sir Peter Scott to build on the ideas of his famous bird sanctuary at Slimbridge and develop a visitor centre and wildfowl attraction. This collection of wooden buildings – the latest has a grass roof – has become a much-loved centre; it is friendly, welcoming and accessible with something for everyone, from keen birdwatcher to the small child who can buy little brown bags of wheat to feed some of the permanent collection.

At Washington, wildfowl watching comes into its own in winter when the centre is full of migratory birds and is always open. This is also a conservation centre, showing through a bright and attractive exhibition how water can be conserved and the importance of wetlands habitats for the species one sees. Their new café (which I helped to develop and design) incorporates regional foods and traditions. The light fresh atmosphere was conceived so that the colours, duck-egg blues and watery greens, would connect and lead to a deck where visitors can sit and watch the birds and view the landscape setting. Among the feast of dishes I researched and suggested were potato cake, a thrifty dish; pan Haggerty, another make-do dish of onions, cheese and potatoes; leek pudding; Panacklety, a beef or bacon fry-up with potatoes. Bramble hinny – Tyneside is the place for hinnies, so named because the cakes, or scones 'sing' as the batter cooks on the griddle and hinny is vernacular for honey – and clootie pudding, a fruit pudding with white rum sauce. This was still served at home with vinegar and pepper on Passion Sunday until the 1950s. Not all these are on the menu, but there are many homely choices such as mince and dumplings, Alnwick stew, bacon stotties, cooked on the griddle to save energy and give its crisp required texture (stottie bread is a local term for a large bread roll), and roasts on Sundays will all keep out the cold.

YORKSHIRE

24

Bolton Abbey Estate
and Priest's House, Barden Tower

North Yorkshire

On one of my visits to the Bolton Abbey estate I walked, without human company, albeit with plenty of friendly fauna, from the bridge at the Cavendish Pavilion to the east bank on a road that runs upwards for a short way, full of primula and fritillary with the Wharfe running along the valley bottom. This was a Wordsworthian view in spring of the river, which is unseen in summer when trees are full.

I climbed up the opposite side through a wall in early evening sunlight with a company of sheep, their offspring and the last of the previous year's pheasants into Low Park, where the indigenous red deer were once kept for the lord's winter table. It now teems with Swaledale sheep. The path travels towards the Valley of Desolation, with some noisy company of the ewes calling their offspring and the abrasive cry of the pheasants, the curlew and the waterfalls; but as William Hazlitt wrote, 'country noises are good noises made comfortable to the ear by the space in which they can vibrate'.

I saw new oaks; a hundred were planted to replace those lost in successive storms although the valley was named about 150 years ago after another such storm. The oak is still king up here; some are hollow, the remnants of what was once a deep forest. There is no desolation today from the wall to the high point of the waterfall at 550 feet. From here you can go on to Simon's Seat, an eight mile walk up to 1550 feet with possibly a view into the valley of Parcevall Hall Gardens. (see page 122) And then on my return on the opposite fell, I saw what appeared to be a team of synchronised gymnasts with large, white arms swinging over and around, over and round – the incongruous sight of a wind farm.

There are further walks up to Barden Tower, once the hunting lodge of Lord Henry Clifford, where the Cliffords feasted after their sport in Barden Forest before returning to Skipton Castle. Together with the castle Lady Anne restored the tower in

1659, where she stayed and enjoyed the 'well wooded vista of Wharfedale'. She also restored the circular hospital built by her mother at Beamsley, just beyond the priory. Although the story of the shepherd Lord Henry who lived among the flocks and his employees, spurning the castle for a simpler life, is the romantic association, the link with Lady Anne Clifford is a no less extraordinary personal battle fought and won against all odds. After Lady Anne's father bequeathed all his estates to his brother, she spent almost sixty years trying to win back what she considered her lawful inheritance. This was large: Skipton, Brougham, Brough, Appleby and Pendragon castles and Barden Tower.

When Anne eventually won back Barden the Civil War was still raging and the Roundheads had taken Wharfedale. Most of the buildings as well as the castles suffered. She rebuilt Barden in 1657 and the almshouses in 1651. It is recorded that she often stayed here and must have entertained a little, being so proud of this restoration that her Skipton guests were always sent over to Barden to see the work. Until the age of 86 she travelled and visited all her properties, including Barden. After her death the estate reverted to the Earls of Cork and Burlington and so is today part of their vast Yorkshire holdings. The tower is open to the elements once more, but the Priest's House next door is where refreshments are and have been traditionally served for probably 100 years when the building was a farmhouse.

When Lady Anne travelled she did not take the easy roads but paid for the gates and hedges to be cut to make way. She travelled from one castle to another, rewarding those who carried her effects, the furniture she took with her. She invited her neighbours at New Year and Christmas, set up repair funds, endowed churches and repaired them. Those who provided music and entertainment were also rewarded. Her manner and style seems to have bridged the divide between the rich and famous, and the poor and hard-working with whom she would sit with the ladies in her almshouses.

The ruins had an unsettling effect on me, perhaps because they are the legacy of such bitter inter-family quarrelling. But the interior of the Priest's House opposite is welcoming, well polished and lit by a flaming fire, much needed in April. A most elegant dresser dominates the room, and the oak beams are silver-grey with age; the dresser bears silver and china and a large fruit bowl. Local game takes pride of place on the menu: hunting lodge pâtés, rabbit casseroles and wild venison all had a seasonal sound, served with fresh vegetables. There is no mean hand in the large bowls of soup served with thick granary bread. Although the scones, they concede, are not made in this kitchen. all the cakes are made on the spot with toasted fruit loaf and Yorkshire curd tart which are welcomed by walkers as testified by a farmer's wife who does bed and breakfast on the estate and who eats here regularly. Other dishes are leek and mushroom bake and smoked fish with blinis which you can sample with Black Sheep ale, local mead and fruit wines.

Food is served in the oak room with its great fireplace, evidently where Lady Anne would inspect her parishioners as they filed past. The tradition of serving teas has continued with just a small break or two for well over a hundred years: one recent tenant, who was the last, a Mrs Bootham, tended this service for some considerable time from one of the farm buildings nearby.

When the Reverend Whitaker first saw Barden standing in 1774, only ninety years after Lady Anne died, it was entire, and then he saw its stripping down to a picturesque ruin. (He was in his own time also a conservationist, having planted 422,000 oaks between 1784 and 1799 at Holme.) Barden once had wild boar feeding off the acorns; the forest administrators under the Lords of Skipton made this their centre. There were wild bee stocks, highly valued and tended by special officers who had the commission of hunting the bees and all their wonderful by-products.

25

Bolton Abbey, Estate and Tea Cottage

North Yorkshire

The virtues of the Bolton Abbey estate are not unsung in Yorkshire, yet I confess I had no suspicion of this embarrassment of riches. I am now captivated by the views, walks and estate in which of the ruins of Bolton Priory lies. This is covered with rich virginia creeper in autumn and in spring it is surrounded by daffodils. Yet Bolton Abbey is a living church framed by what appears to be an infinite landscape. Truly this is a centre for a whole Wharfedale discovery.

The Reverend Whitaker, whose great work The History of Craven chronicled every parish in the region, put it well: this is a 'sequestered scene'. The abbey or priory 'stands in a beautiful curvature of the Wharfe, on a level sufficiently elevated to protect from its inundation and low enough for every purpose of picturesque effect'. For Whitaker, Bolton fared better when compared with Fountains. He thought the Wharfe to be more magnificent than the Skell, and could not find Bolton's equal in the North although he accepted that the ruins of Fountains made a better study.

When Whitaker first saw Bolton in the late eighteenth-century the trees were closer to the priory, elms, ash and oak, all the ingredients for a Turner landscape, whose view of 1809 hangs in the British Museum. And now this is a late twentieth-century escape, with an aspect, sounds and taste, which cannot be bettered. Virtually all this is open and accessible to visitors, stretching to the horizon from the Tea Cottage courtyard, near the small cluster of cottages and former village shop. A glance through the Hole in the Wall bordering the road is only the beginning. Be prepared, for there are walks enough to fill up a week: a ruined hunting tower at Barden, with good food, a small farmhouse, where teas and miniature trains are run together and all managed separately by tenants of the Bolton Abbey estate. About 120 years ago tourism burgeoned here as visitors came by rail, although the estate has been a favourite pleasure ground of the West Riding for more than 200 years. Lucky Bradford and

Leeds folk have this virtually at the back door. A visitor caveat: Bolton Abbey Estate can be very busy on hot Sundays and bank holidays.

Long before the plundering Vikings arrived the Dales had attracted religious foundations – which later the Normans helped to re-establish. Bolton Priory was founded on land given by Lady Alicia of Skipton by the monks from Embsay in 1145; it was an Augustinian priory which, in contrast to the Cistercian order, had good relations with the community whom the canons taught and preached among. They opened hospitals and mingled with the community who worshipped in their churches. Their income for building and maintenance came from the lead mines. The abbey tower, built by Prior Richard Moone in 1520, was not finished at the Dissolution and although lead was taken from the roof and furnishings were stolen, worship continued in the nave. The estate was then sold to the Cliffords. Whitaker rather resented restoration and wrote: 'I must protest against that miserable taste which can level the floor of a conventional church to a bowling green and clear up the area which surrounds it with the spruceness of a modern pleasure ground.'

With the Gothic revival in the 1850s two eminent Victorian architects, Augustus Pugin and George Street, embellished and restored Bolton: glass by the former, pews, font and sanctuary and the east wall by the latter. The nave shows how the roof with its golden angels might have looked. The ogee arch in the west porch is magnificent and a nineteenth-century painted wall has filled in the gap which would have been the rood screen, with the choir beyond. Victorian symbolist work, delicately depicting plants and fruit, was decorated by local craftsmen. Further Victorian decoration is evident in Pugin's south windows which narrate the Gospels. Today Bolton Priory is a testament of faith and continuity which, despite a catalogue of difficulties, now has a lively congregation.

There are many walks and dedicated paths over the moors, but the Wharfe is the draw flowing through the estate. It attracts one and charms, whatever the season. Wharfedale is the longest Yorkshire dale, running from the source at Oughtershaw twenty-five miles above down to the Ouse below York. Once these moors were the hunting grounds – deer forests – of the Lords of Skipton Castle. They were then inherited by the Devonshires who culti-vated the celebrated grouse moors. The estate is a very fine mix-ture of moorland, sheep farming, woodland and meadows. And a kind of corporate, or perhaps country, image is reassuring where every estate building farm, barn or house is well cared for, the paintwork, always a pleasant buff green signifies, their belonging. The walks have a number of natural high points, Simon's Seat, and the Strid which was opened up for public view-ing by William Carr in the late eighteenth century, with strategic seats for the best views.

The Strid is a fast running gorge through which the Wharfe passes on its journey through woods full of flowers in spring with snowdrops, celandine, primroses and bluebells looking set to flower in May. It has its own folklore. The mixed woodland of larch, fir and oaks connects it with the Dales Way and I first had this view from the terrace of the delightful and pertinently named Tea Cottage whose mullioned windows look on to the moors on both sides of the river. Roses really run around the door of the stone cottage and over a rustic arch, and pergolas are covered with pink geraniums. And the perfume of wallflowers permeates the paths. Only a short walk along, curving the other side of the wall beyond the cottage to the priory with a perfect view from the bridge, the Wharfe sparkles.

On my first visit I put the world to rights in the company of a seriously well-travelled local man from Ilkley, he with his newspa-per and a coffee, and I with lunch on the terrace. He told me that he had walked in South Africa, Australia and heaven knows where, yet of all his walks, for him these moors were the best. He was from down the road and yet glued to his seat on that terrace with its dress-circle views of the Dales.

The Tea Cottage was probably part of a tithe barn dating from the late eighteenth century. The first floor has a large oak tie beam that sat above the dividing wall of the former two cot-tages where estate workers lived. There are fresh flowers and lamps on the polished tables, a stone flagged floor, and all is spot-less. This is no lacy place, bentwood chairs and white paint pre-dominate throughout five small rooms, some with small wrought-iron fireplaces, leading invitingly one out of the other, with a large room on the first floor that gives you the best view. Crawl under a beam and sit on a settle and look beyond. I like the Tea Cottage at all times because the combination of situation and the food that Mrs Barker, who bakes and oversees, is right. There is enough choice for anyone's palate.

There is iced Earl Grey tea in the summer, local roast meats, poached salmon cold with scones and tea for high tea (this erstwhile repast is alive and steaming in Yorkshire). Here it includes mouth-watering lemon meringue pie among the cakes displayed on a stand, cream teas, dependable scones or roast chicken, and comforting omelettes and grills for those who want to stoke up for a long walk. The Yorkshire curd tart was moist and curdy, and

the coffee was good and hot. I have sat on the terrace surrounded the borage-driven bees in late autumn, yet find the interior cool on a summer's day. This intimate and charming situation would be the perfect place for an assignation. And it is not just for crinklies, younger visitors also respect quality: three young Yorkshire lads were tucking into super sausages on the morning of my third visit.

26

Boroughbridge and Norton Conyers

North Yorkshire

Boroughbridge is a good town and position for a decision; from here one could take the road north east to Coxwold and the North Yorkshire moors or across a plateau to the Dales and Pateley Bridge. One could even make the next stop Blanchland, the Wall, Durham and Northumberland. Once Boroughbridge was in the West Riding, now it is in North Yorkshire. But the town has been subjected to more than boundary changes. Dynasties have been fought for and lost here: the Duke of Lancaster was defeated here in 1322 by Edward II, subsequently beheaded for his treason.

The history goes much futher back as there are prehistoric monoliths, the Devils' Arrows, three large standing stones, which predate the Roman town of Aldborough a mile or so away. Boroughbridge is an intact market town, proud of its history and traditions and reassuringly thriving. Aldborough, was a Roman settlement, Isurium Brigantum, built on the site of a Brigantes camp. Leland saw the Roman pavements in 1534. Was this the same journey as Ribchester?

Boroughbridge has two very elegant squares: St James' Square and Hall Square, with its Tuscan columned market cross, large and quite imposing in this context and scale of the surrounding buildings. Both squares are cobbled with a mix of refined white-washed houses with deep pantile roofs, some in brick from clay dug nearby and a very worthwhile array of small shops selling everything one needs. If you fancy a greengrocer, where the pavement display is as near an art form as you can get, Boroughbridge is the place, and there are two bakers worth a visit. At Thompsons, local burnished red-gold shallots hang alongside carrots and onions like eighteenth-century swags; onions, potatoes, celeriac and baskets of fecund pumpkins, heralding Hallowe'en. What better sight on a cold bright autumnal morning. Localness is celebrated on the chalk board. In summer the vegetables and fruit include raspberries and blackcurrants and another greengrocer on a wonderful corner site has an incised and painted pattern in the reveal above the door.

I discovered that Miss Mudd, whose Edwardian dairy business won prizes and is well represented in Pateley Bridge museum (see page 143), ran the dairy in Aldborough for forty-five years from 1910. She also entertained celebrities, winning prizes for her butter and cheeses at shows all over the country, becoming internationally famous. Even today Miss Mudd is indirectly linked to events, for the dairy hosts the Aldborough festival. In 1913, moreover, a Mr Nicholson also served the community of Aldborough in every degree; he ran the village shop, had a yeast round, taking this crucial ingredient to the villages within seven miles and opened virtually all hours. Whoever thought late-opening shops were a new phenomenon should note that village shops did and still do really serve their community. Mr Nicholson's shop opened at 7am and closed at 9pm and 11pm on Saturdays, and if this was not service enough, he took people to the Boroughbridge station in his pony and trap, driving others to dances and whist drives in his wagonette as well as keeping horses, cows, hens and pigs.

Aldborough still has a maypole, put up 1903 and to this day danced around whenever May Day now falls; once the children used to practise every evening in late April. On May Day they 'looked like angels' and danced until they dropped against the sound of the church bells. The 1960s scrapbook in which this was recorded is kept like a treasure in the library.

Another conflict, about 350 years later than Boroughbridge, the Civil War battle of Marston Moor has left an unusual mark at Norton Conyers, an interesting house found on the way to Masham and the Dales. Its most famous association is a literary one with Charlotte Brontë. Her visit here in 1839, when she was a governess was a possible inspiration for Jane Eyre. For Charlotte described Mr Rochester's house as 'three storeys high of proportions not vast, though considerable', just as Norton Conyers is today, with an exceptional pedigree that can be traced back to the Domesday Book. First the home of a Norman family, Conyers, it changed hands in the fourteenth century when the Norton family bought the house and estate, changing again when the Nortons turned against the Crown in 1569. Through marriage to the successors, the Musgrave family, the house came into the Graham family, who live here still.

The first Sir Richard Graham was a staunch supporter of the royalist cause, and was possibly wounded at the battle of Marston Moor. His horse managed to carry back his wounded master, right to the house, walked through the hall and mounted the stairs leaving a hoof mark, or rather hot shoe imprint. This has now been removed to the landing to save other foot falls wearing it away. This is a heroic legend.

Norton Conyers feels Gothic yet the gable ends are distinctly seventeenth-century; older timbers of the fifteenth century have been found in the attics. The house is settled very well in a composed position, looking out to soft parkland. The large full-height hall leading to the famous stair is panelled and hung with portraits, one by Sir Peter Lely, views of the house and park and one by John Ferneley picturing the whole hunt when the master of the Quorn Hunt was Sir Bellingham Graham.

The principal door from the park has a rusticated porch like that at Nunnington Hall. The ha-ha is nearby, the parkland level offering a very tranquil aspect. In the walled garden, which is truly like a secret garden, fruit grows magnificently. The soft fruits attain a gargantuan size and intensity of taste. As we tasted the raspberries and walked around tasting we all agreed the last always tasted the best. How long does one go on tasting? The gardens are a tantalising mêlée of wide borders, with foxgloves and artichokes, far-reaching fennel, alchilla and scabious, exuberant show-off peonies and lilies all cheek by jowl, but not in competition. One encounters height, depth, taste and colour. An apple tree is entwined with a rambler rose, white Bobby James. The red-currants were begging to be gathered; bushes were bending under the weight of the fruit almost the size of grapes. There are peaches - and this is the North – in the hothouse, a charming flat-roofed eighteenth-century orangery. You can pick your own organic fruit and some of the unusual hardy plants are for sale.

Norton Conyers has a catalogue of design styles reflecting each generation's flirtation with the latest fashion. The eighteenth-century stables are an important example of their period; they were designed by William Bellwood who worked under

Robert Adam at Newby Hall and are listed. The coach house became a garage in 1911 when the present owner's grandmother was the first woman to drive a car in North Yorkshire. There is a charming 1930s garden room, also a rare example, where simple teas are served on charity open days. All this makes Norton Conyers an approachable house, not large, not too grand and in the process of restoration, but nonetheless a very singular visit.

27

Botton Village: Skinningrove and Staithes

North Yorkshire

Y ou may have to enquire several times for the way to this hidden area where Botton village is located. Danby Dale is right
in the North York Moors and Park. Botton is a 'new' Camphill village founded in 1955 and is attached to an older settlement. The
new buildings relate in their own particular manner to the nineteenth-century vernacular cottages, but the history of this valley
haven running off the River Esk goes back much further to the
foundation of Rosedale Abbey. The monks travelled through the
dale to Whitby, and the Quakers also came here in the seventeenth century to avoid the prejudice their form of worship
attracted. Camphill, like the Quakers, also gained strength from
the tranquillity of the setting. The Camphill community is almost
self-sufficient, living with disabled people and working the land
for mutual benefit. People who have learning difficulties can
thrive and grow in this energy-giving environment; they con-
tribute to the community at large and to their visitors who buy
the food and wonderful crafts they make.

Dr Karl König founded the village in 1955, since when the
community has grown and acquired more land so that stock and
food can be reared and produced by the residents. Botton is well
endowed with traditional village ingredients: a food shop, bookshop, bakery, coffee shop, meeting place and of course the
church, which are surrounded by the farms, market gardens and
forestry.

This village grows its food biodynamically: for example,
mixed crops are grown to discourage predators from the main
crop. They farm according to traditional husbandry, through
crop rotation and harnessing the peak forces of energy – seasons,
light and time. Their principles are organic, without additives or
hormones, using the natural energy of the plant, and the growing year follows time-honoured patterns. The celebration of seasons and festivals is fundamental to the social ethic of the community where the church is pivotal. Music, dancing, drama, the
land; these are all inextricably linked, as is the architecture,

which stems from the Expressionistic movement in Germany to which Rudolf Steiner, whose philosophy König followed, was a proponent. Botton's church is a good example of this organic form, of which metamorphosis is the most recognisable element.

There are no angles to the church: the building flows, yet contains paradoxically geometrical forces. The east end has a rectilinear hip roof which dips down from the frames, while the apse curves up following the horizon of Danby High Moor. In fact everything moves or curves, including the entrance porch. The window reveals bring the landscape right into the building. It is built in rough-sawn timber and stone, with wooden door handles, and the eaves and frames are picked out in blue. Other buildings such as the Dolls Workshop are constructed in the same Expressionistic idiom, where the window frames are picked out in red. Inside I met residents who were busily making dolls with brown and cream faces for sale on their forthcoming open day, a highlight in the community calender. Stillness and concentration surrounded the residents and co-workers who were carding, weaving and stitching. And the whole visit had a background of running water, from a tributary of the Esk, as well as birdsong and the sound of building. There is always an air of renewal in these villages.

Such meanderings are energising, and an almost-ready field of cultivated raspberries had me imagining a long-lost, powerful taste which, if you are not there in July, you can bring back captured in a bottle of their quite wonderful jam. Taking another direction, a walk skirting the bottom of a field will sharpen your appetite for the bakery, where I bought a stoneground loaf from the groaning racks of warm loaves, the air heavy with a hot yeasty aroma. Another workshop was filled with the fragrance of jam making. It was gooseberry on that day. At the shop all the preserves and conserves are on sale where I took a bottle or two of the most tart, moist and thick marmalade; this is good enough to eat with a spoon! Good marmalade, I believe is worthy of a system of appellation, like wine.

Danby is in the fosilliferous region where alum was once mined; it is an informal village which centres round a green where the sheep graze freely; this extends to fields of harebells, a mill, stone walls and the sound of water. The Danes lived here, and in the Middle Ages the merchants brought salt, grain, fish and jet across here from Whitby, while wool and flour were taken back. The church has a wooden thirteenth-century balcony which has been restored by Temple Moore. The churchyard gives a 280 degree view of steep roads, leading to the rolling moor tops with their ridges, furrows and hummocks, and the valley paths are waymarked with sharp white lettering on dark green.

I took the road recommended, to Skinningrove, through the heather with a purple haze to a most curious seaside former industrial village. This lies in a gap between the cliffs which now form part of the Cleveland Way. The industry was the smelting of iron ore and fishing, but there is little left of the fishing story – just the detritus of Lobster pots on the shingle, miners' allotments growing in the side of the cliff bank at right angles with pigeon coops, wooden sheds and a calm sea. But a small private museum commemorates the iron mined and the men who laboured here. The coastline has something for everyone: walkers, painters, people messing about on the sands. Next, Staithes is a must, an untouched time-aside fishing port, where Dame Laura Knight painted.

Staithes is not really in the grasp of the tourist, it is still cobbled and was the home of the coble boat, a relation of the Norwegian 'pram'. The newer housing at the top gives no hint of the enclosed dark-stone houses knitted close together in the village below, surrounding a harbour. A steep lane leads to the port, but it is not worth trying to motor down to the harbour where I bought a fresh crab sandwich.

Here in 1945 women were still dressed in their traditional black skirts, cream blouses, gloves and contrasting white bonnets. But I discovered that the Staithes bonnet is still made today. This piece of headgear has a pleated frill at the back, but its singularity is the colour change which denotes the different stages in a woman's life: coloured and sprigged for the young and married, black for those in mourning for a year, and purple for the second year. They reverted to light colours when the mourning was over. I heard that the last lady to wear a bonnet every time she went out in the village died just two years ago, but the female staff in the post office wear them today; a twentieth-century conversion of an eighteenth-century workwear and an equally attractive use. The writer Gerald du Maurier was intrigued enough with the different colours and shapes, frilly for women, high-crowned for men, to direct that the male cast should wear these in his play Trilby.

There is an unusual pregnant atmosphere in Staithes which with the cliff and sea encouraged artists to settle and paint here in the 1920s. I would like to have seen it with its army of fishing boats, although a few still work out of this harbour. I would also like to have seen it before the wooden bridge was replaced by concrete. Picture this backwater, as a harbour, teeming with hundreds of cobles – Staithes had 400 of these flat-bottomed fishing craft, the northern equivalent to the Cornish lugger. They sailed out to catch lobster and crab while the larger craft took the cod with nets. Staithes may be small, but its fishing fleet once dwarfed that of its neighbour Whitby, my next port of call.

28

Brompton and Bridlington, the Wolds and Weaverthorpe

East Yorkshire

I wanted to make an early Wordsworth connection and managed this by visiting Gallows Hill near Brompton, west of Scarborough, before I travelled to the Lake counties. The church is part of a literary pilgrimage where the small paper licence fixed inside reads: 'William Wordsworth, gentleman of Grasmere in the county of Westmorland, married by licence to Mary Hutchinson in 1802.'

The fields between Scarborough and Pickering, and then on to the road I travelled to Masham, were described more than 200 years ago as ings, 'low-lying mowing ground' now growing peas, potatoes, and other superb crops in the black alluvion over blue clay soil. Brompton lies in a pleasant valley among the mole-brown wolds; in autumn the hedges in need are of a darn, and there are few trees between the newly ploughed fields. As Dorothy Wordsworth once said, these are 'swelling grounds, and sometime a single tree or clump of trees'. She and William had walked from Grasmere to Brompton: 'On Friday morning July 10th 1802 William and I set forward to Keswick on our road to Gallows Hill', preceding the marriage later that autumn.

The Wordsworths walked a good deal and sometimes took a coach, arriving on July 15 having taken cakes and wine at a farmhouse near Bolton Castle; they also saw Helmsley Castle. On their return, they wondered at the ruins of Rievaulx, where they had nothing except some boiled milk and bread at an 'exquisitely-neat farmhouse' (how I search for these). It is well known that Dorothy could not bring herself to go to the wedding. She languished dejectedly in her bedroom, only coming downstairs to greet them after they returned from the church.

A visit to All Saints, Brompton, with its proud buttressed-porch and an interesting doorway, even with interior changes, is obligatory. The small twelfth-century church has an octagonal spire, a wide nave with three bays, fifteenth-century arches and a thirteenth-century chancel. The spire is short in comparison with the tower and there are unusually fat diagonal buttresses. The interior stone flooring was replaced with wood block, the east window was reduced and the organ case is by Temple Moore, but the church's fame owes a little to the Wordsworth marriage certificate now looking insignificant on the vestry wall. And outside the daffodils, in their prime time, made the picture complete.

Another monument was raised in the church to a local farmer, Richard Sawdon, who died in 1782. His diary, like Parson Woodforde's, is consumed with details of food, albeit in rather humourless note-like vein. He set out for London on July 10, 1758. His first stop was Malton and he arrived on July 19. During the first three Yorkshire days from Brompton to Doncaster he consumed a couple of rabbits and fowls at Malton, boiled salmon and a couple of roasted fowls at York for supper. He breakfasted and dined with friends on what we are not told, but at Ferrybridge later, at four, he consumed two more rabbits, and 'beef stakes with tarts; jellies etc., as usual'. Later, 'Same evening at Doncaster suped on roast fowls, ham, & green pease: and next day dined upon mutton chops, and rost Ducks & drank tea'. Dorothy's travelling fuel seems frugal after this.

Brompton village is worth a wander. There is a peaceful aspect with rows of stone cottages with a farm selling free-range eggs near the River Sawdon. After a quarter of an hour towards Sledmere, travelling through perfect, gentle lanes with the wolds looking like a rolled-out bolt of brown corduroy, I saw a Norman tower on the horizon. I stopped and found myself being invited to join in afternoon Evensong at St Andrew's at Weaverthorpe. This has a graceful tower, with a round projecting staircase. The interior was restored by G E Street with the patronage of Sir Tatton Sykes. The drum-shaped font is also Norman and Street added a charming wooden lych gate. This was an exceptional moment. I was immediately part of that tiny congregation as the vicar invited me to stay, hoping that the last hymn would be a favourite.

I arrived late at Sewerby Hall on the outskirts of Bridlington which is divided into old and new, right at the far end of the town, and where you meet the house and park facing the North Sea, at the end of the garden, sitting in a park, complete with its own bowls and cricket pitch, formal and walled gardens. Sewerby Hall, now a museum, which first opened in 1936, is one of those informal delights, where the character shines through. The attendants attend and proudly regale you with stories. The whole setting is a pleasure from the Georgian house, with its story of Henrietta Maria who had traded in her possessions and pictures when she landed after the Restoration to pay for her passage, and safety, right through to the poignant sound of 'Amy, beautiful Amy'. This enchanting and very much now a period song filters down the corridors, mingling, playing continuously in the background, quite surreal; Amy Johnson was a local girl and her story is told here.

Late on a Saturday afternoon I was the only visitor and found an entertaining helping of this music, the cutting edge sculpture, art and the seventeenth-century portraits on the staircase. As for live music, a very civilised series of lunchtime recitals takes place every Thursday. This is to be expanded. Local pianists perform on the restored Blüther complementing the furniture collection. And I understand that the audience arrives fairly thick as the standard is high. When I walked around these gardens among immense monkey puzzle trees with different levels and stone seats, I half expected to hear the sound of a distant band playing in the Victorian garden. I also heard that the cricket teas, on Saturdays in the summer, in the pleasure grounds' pavilion are renowned. I gather the food features, butter cream sponges, coffee, lemon and chocolate, and cheese scones, sausages, and a pot of tea at suitable outdoor prices.

The rolling wolds between here and Sledmere are called boy's land because the soil is so easy to till. Among the villages and small agricultural towns Pocklington has a fair and Market Weighton has the oldest racecourse in the world and, since 1519 has hosted the longest running race. It is held on the third Thursday in March, the prize money includes the income from a sum invested in 1618 by Lord Burlington. At Great Driffield I found one of those rare market town hotels where roasts, pies and, good vegetables are served, the sort of hostelry where the town seems to meet up on a Saturday night. I felt I was getting nearer to that ideal of a country hotel, one reads about where one hopes to see a spread table of cold sirloin cut in delicate slices, done to a turn, potatoes swimming with butter, the perfection of an apple pie, sweet yet tart, sitting under a blanket of yellow cream with instantly melting pastry, and ripe Stilton and some good wine.

29

Cusworth Hall, Doncaster

South Yorkshire

Cusworth Hall was a Georgian country house which has become the home of the Museum of South Yorkshire Life. It is a bonus visit, opening all year and cossetting all comers even on damp, dull late November days, when other historic properties have been 'put to bed'. It is often the first historic halt on my way north in Yorkshire. Cusworth may need and certainly deserves a large dose of tender loving restoration, but it has a good heart and atmosphere. These attributes prevailed, by all accounts, in the days when the Battie-Wrightsons, a family which gained a reputation for looking after their staff and estate were living there. Today Cusworth still retains that focus in the local scene.

This house was built in the classical style between 1740 and 1748. It has a stately facade with curving wings on either side; one contained the coaches, the other the great kitchen and domestic offices. Two curving staircases lead up to the main front door. The south front was extended and remodelled by James Paine, and the north, soon hopefully to be restored, by George Platt. Inside a long colonnaded hall one senses a soupcon of country house elegance. Fewer ferns, admittedly, than the Edwardian images in the guide book, but there is a piano, many pictures and a warming fire to welcome winter callers. Each of the principal rooms now displays much of the social history collection. The library, shortly to be restored, has an intriguing Chinese-like fretwork bookcase which provenance has been recently attributed to John Rawstorne of about 1795.

Georgian details abound in the main reception rooms: the marble fireplace, the painted breakfast room ceiling and the classical chapel. Joseph Rose worked on the shell plasterwork (see page 134). Pictures are hung on the staircase, and one reminds you that the North's most famous racecourse is outside the town and where the St Leger has been run since 1776. On the attractive well-lit landing large glass-fronted cases at eye level give the impression of shopfronts; one, as a hatshop window, is brimming with shapes, colours, materials and styles ranging from the 1870s to the 1940s. One really does have a chicken's head by way of decoration. In one of the smaller first-floor rooms, there is a costume collection of eighteenth and nineteenth-century and some twentieth-century pieces, with a 1950s circular skirt for rock'n'roll buffs. But I coveted a particularly beautiful nineteenth-century grey-blue cloak with a tartan lining.

The original kitchen has been filled with artefacts and furniture of the Victorian period, yet it is an eighteenth-century space of double height and shuttered windows. When these were opened they would show approaching guests to the butler. A lovely long table had me yearning to cook, and an enormous dresser with a carved cornice was filled with a collection of creamware; there is a sumptuous collection of Don ware in Doncaster Museum itself. Next door I was shown a preparation room with a bread oven which they hope to rejuvenate. To the south is the country park with fine rolling landscape and a commanding view, where today in the spirit of a former age when grand tea parties were laid out, country park fairs and assemblies enliven the grounds.

Cusworth's curators have drawn on the experiences and memories of the last serving staff in a fascinating small publication, Caring for Cusworth. The memoirs date from the first decades of this century when the family, reduced to only one member, William Henry Battie-Wrightson, who lived alone yet maintained the grander way of life. Indeed a full complement of staff was employed to look after the owner and estate. For example there were five gardeners, a housekeeper, a cook and nine maids; hours were long but the atmosphere was happy. By breakfast all the principal rooms would have been tidied, fireplaces swept out, grates blackened and hearths whitened with pipe clay. After this, there was silver and brass cleaning and dusting as well as a rolling programme of cleaning duties and tasks; carpets to be beaten after sprinkling with tea leaves to keep the dust at bay, the kitchen floor to be scrubbed daily and so on.

Mr Battie-Wrightson was more than a mere employer, he expected hard work but respected his staff who were given four breaks a day, with ham for breakfast and fresh bread for Saturday tea. Generosity prevailed and Cusworth was self-sufficient; fruit and vegetables were grown here, game came from the park, hams hung in the passage, bread was baked and fruit was turned into jams and curds. Cook also made pies and potted meats. You can still find potted meats in butchers' shops up here, usually eaten for 'tea'. Any surplus was sent to the grocers Hodgson and Hepworth in Doncaster. Doncaster market still has a good reputation with locals; there are twenty fish stalls with supplies coming from the east coast, and game dealers sell venison and pheasant in the feather.

The staff who came back in 1982 to recall their memories spoke of Mr Wrightson's menu: partridge on toast, boiled salmon with homemade crisps – game chips – and accompanied with cucumber. Another remembered shooting party luncheons of jugged hare, blackcurrant jelly and a whole York ham. These recollections colour a benevolent picture of a man who insisted his servants wore their own clothes when they went out, who donated a bottle of port or sherry for their hall evenings and who held sports days for the staff and their families. He took them on holiday when he went away and marked festivals; at Easter he gave each one an egg 'laid' in a china cup and saucer. Staff also enjoyed the estate, learned tennis and rowed on the lake.

If you can manage a visit to Brodsworth Hall, a stone's throw away, you will find a contrasting style and period – nineteenth-century architecture. Life at Brodsworth was more formal, yet the long corridors of staff bedrooms on the upper floor were quite evocative of life in a lino setting. The food, however, and the service in the tea room is managed by the same caterers as at Cusworth and is equally good. At Brodsworth they have introduced a touch of elegance, bringing the food that you have chosen out to you in the garden.

I have had many pleasant interludes at Cusworth. The family feel is just as tangible in the Hall tea room where a second fire was glowing in an iron basket when I had lunch one November. The uneven cobbled floor, together with the mahogany shop counters filled acceptably with some nostalgia, are also genuine. There is marvellous value, extremely friendly staff and very acceptable food. A liberal slice of country bloomer bread, white or granary is served with seasonal leek and potato soup or with cheese and they make their substantial sandwiches with good ham.

A wide selection of cakes is baked in the tiniest of kitchens by staff who like their work: coffee sponge, little mincemeat patties, moist and light apricot and orange cake, lemon cake, date and walnut bread for the sweet-toothed. There are four varieties of scones: plain, cheese, fruit and date and walnut and there is no close season for the teacakes and crumpets, normally only in the shops in autumn when I was a child, while comforting plates of cheese on toast can always be ordered. A stylish terracotta bowl of fruit, no lonely golden delicious here, is one of several distinctive touches along with a menu design which complements the good coffee. The staff wait at table and one suspects Mr Wrightson would approve of them as they are beautifully turned out. Happily, this is a coach house tea-room which has not been over-customised. But, quite importantly, for Cusworth is attractive to families who can spend time in the extensive grounds as well as the house, children are catered for with half portions.

On the terrace one finds seats to sit on and eat or gaze over-looking the park where you may only be a few miles from the city, but, in terms of civility and tranquillity, worlds away.

30

Fountains Abbey, Ripon

North Yorkshire

The ruins of Fountains Abbey provide one of the most beautiful sights in England. But this excursion is a mix of ruin and a modern centre. For at least 300 years, hundreds of thousands of visitors have been converging to the wooded Skell valley where the remains of Fountains Abbey have inspired them to wonder. It lies in a timeless Yorkshire landscape. It is a blend of 800-year-old medieval monasticism, eighteenth-century water gardens with classical temples, a sixteenth-century honey stone house, and lastly a High Victorian Gothic church by William Burges. For thousands of years this landscape has also been subjected to religious and secular manipulation. Now there is a late twentieth-century addition.

In 1992 a new centre was built to provide refreshment, a shop and a gateway to the ruins of the abbey. I suspect the building will be a cause célèbre for some years to come. But the new engages with the past and, if you know what to look for, you can interpret some of the associations. Here I can, for once, satisfy those who ask for more modern buildings. Just as John Aislabie used the ruins to make his version of the Picturesque in the early eighteenth century, so the new building has been conceived to frame the ruins through two L-shaped wings surrounding a new large courtyard space, with fast-maturing planting screening the road.

Fountains Abbey was founded in 1132 by a breakaway group of the Benedictine order which wanted to revert to a basic form of devotion. They settled here in the land between the Furness Abbey cell and the Augustinians at Bolton Priory. The location was ideal: limestone was readily available, the terrain makes for good grass and good grazing (the monks made creamy Yorkshire cheeses from ewes' milk), and the Skell provided the water for washing, brewing and drainage.

Eventually Fountains was to become part of the powerful Cistercian order ruled from Rome; what marks this order is the separation with the church divided by screens to keep the choir and lay monks apart, just as the magnificent west range would

111

also have been partitioned, dividing the lay clergy from the monks. The lay brethren were the servants; the monks had no day-to-day tasks to perform and they hired agricultural labour. But life was rigorous, there was small comfort, no communication other than sign language and the diet was basic. Hygiene was strict; washing places, cellars, infirmaries and guest houses all show the importance of order in daily lives as well as devotion. The Cistercians became the most economically successful order. They changed the country profoundly, cultivating granges or sheep pastures, which produced riches beyond belief. Venetian and Florentine merchants paid in cash for wool and they even bought the twelfth-century equivalent to quota, speculating on futures.

The path to the abbey crosses a field with no more than a glimpse of the tower, then gradually as you descend from the centre through each level, so another vista comes into the view ahead. As the centre fades out of view it becomes no more than a vernacular roof, it just grows away and then at last Prior Huby's tower confronts you. For me the monumental elements are the marvellous west front doorway, a voussoir with a six springing arched entrance in weathered sandstone quarried on the site (the Nidderdale marble was nearby); and the west range, probably one of the most overwhelming monastic spaces anywhere, vaulting and aisles, laid bare but intact enough to overwhelm the viewer. In the south range, where the refectory was sited at right angles to the cloister, one sees a warming room with its vast fireplace, the reredorter, wash house, is built over the river, but Cistercians kept their architecture and lifestyle devoid of decoration.

Fountains did not survive the Dissolution, but was incorporated into the seventeenth century by John Aislabie. He inherited the estate in 1699 and set about constructing an unsurpassed water garden, inspired by the French gardener Le Notre. The principal design component or main axis is the river, so water replaces the parterre form as a means of division, around which lawns, rustic bridges, and cascades were planned. Aislabie used the ruins and the spire of Ripon to create monumental vistas, completed by his son in a less formal style. William Aislabie bought the ruins of Fountains and the Hall and created one of the first models of the Picturesque by incorporating the rocks and wild features for dramatic effect, becoming the frame or introduction the ruins of the abbey.

Why not look at the new centre and try to find references to the ruins? On returning, you should be reminded of the ruins of the twelfth century through the design of the new architectural forms. The prow-like eave, noted in its full height on the return journey from the abbey is the most memorable design image. It is fractured, yet straight and recalls the ruined east window of the abbey; the pattern of the twelfth-century stone tiles which are early Cistercian can be recalled in the new courtyard. And the vaulting of the marvellous west range are echoed in the curved beams of the restaurant. The new materials are chosen to reflect the light produced by the restaurant's roof angles, an autograph of the architect, Edward Cullinan. The shape of the roof is more reminiscent of the hull of a schooner moulded with lead. It is covered with reclaimed mill tiles, while the rugged base of the stone walls will remind visitors of vernacular barns seen on their journey to the site. The interior offers further references; the overlapping timbers are held by red, blue and green battens, inspired by the interior of William Burges' church.

So, in a place with its fair share of wood, glass and stainless steel, in an area with a reputation for good produce, what is the food like? There is some Yorkshire emphasis and they try to use local suppliers. Sunday roasts with well cooked, not overcooked vegetables do well; Yorkshire damp gingerbread, Ripon spice bread (Ripon also has a nineteenth-century recipe for chicken with two types of stuffing and a cake to celebrate All Hallows, so called cake night), Wensleydale and Coverdale cheeses are to hand, as well as scones. The staff serve the hot dishes, but as most of the food is self-selected, bread and cheese have cellophane wraps, not the best medium for the cheese. One element I like about this restaurant is that I can take a salad, still on offer at five o'clock, which makes a late walk possible. And although the prices may seem a little higher than the rest of the region there is a well thought-out choice for children.

Like the Hon John Byng, an eighteenth-century excursionist

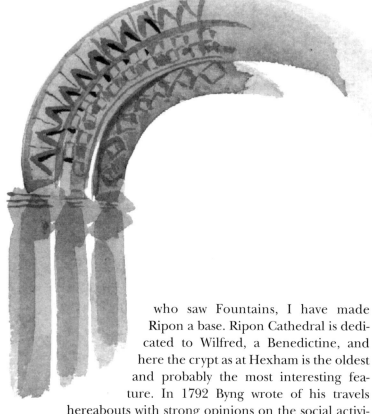

who saw Fountains, I have made Ripon a base. Ripon Cathedral is dedicated to Wilfred, a Benedictine, and here the crypt as at Hexham is the oldest and probably the most interesting feature. In 1792 Byng wrote of his travels hereabouts with strong opinions on the social activities of the area. He dined well on roast fowl at Ripon but did not like chops fried in butter. He escaped to Studley gardens to avoid a noisy fair. Byng liked the landscape; nature was 'bountiful in furnishing hill, vale and wood of fine growth and charming stream', yet he criticised Aislabie's gardens and the fact that there was no shelter for the horses, describing them as 'tricked out with temples and statuary, and a 'paltry Gothic temple'. But 'oh what a beauty and perfection of ruin!!' he wrote of the abbey, but the steeple too 'spruce' and he railed against the removing of rubbish (fallen masonry). He wrote that if it had not been raining he would have stayed longer. On returning to Ripon he 'heated' himself with coffee and toast after a brandy. But this 'survey', he ventures, needs another day.

31

Howden

East Yorkshire

I like to take the A1 northwards to Yorkshire, because it allows me to see the differences in the landscape, which are impossible from an anonymous motorway corridor. But you will have to hurry to see the vestiges of the erstwhile Great North Road which has almost disappeared.

I was aiming for Sledmere in the Yorkshire Wolds, but had the notion to visit Howden whose 138-foot minster tower beckoned across the flat fields. If you want an inkling of what market towns were like without a multiplicity of multiples, this is the one. Howden is situated in the gap of the River Humber into which every river in the East Riding flows between the Lincolnshire and Yorkshire Wolds. Give yourself two hours or so for the architecture and more for the minster, for there is no heavy hand of misdirected planning here. The winding streets survive without touristy tat although Howden is conscious of its built heritage. Some buildings are neglected but I am happy with the town, slightly dusty, I would not wish to see it polished.

Howden's early fame and fortune grew because of the minster then with agriculture and one of the largest horse sales in the country which attracted dealers from all over the continent. Its agricultural roots are apparent in the ancillary buildings behind the small houses. But there are unspoilt nineteenth-century shop fronts, narrow lanes and small squares; even the neglected buildings have their place. This is a lived-in workaday town, which, in spite of losing its horse fair, has elements of prosperity. As I approach this county, from the south, I picture Howden with its discreet charm as a gateway to one of the richest agricultural districts of Yorkshire, becoming richer in the eighteenth century when drainage was introduced and farmers harvested twice over from the same acreage. The wealth must have triggered the good Georgian and Victorian houses and two associated market areas.

Each 'gate' and street should be studied; these show the town's development and growth. Churchside, for example, has a smattering of both eighteenth and nineteenth-century styles.

One cheerful inhabitant, who visits the minster every day, and who would have willingly given me the whole afternoon of history, told me about the hordes of incoming horse dealers. And there is a useful town guide which gives information on the professional classes, the churches, buildings and their occupants. Like others Howden had its own maltster, many inns – more than twenty – a grand Wesleyan chapel and quite exceptional town houses. Several of the porches have a grandeur, while the dressings and decoration display the craft of the builder and stonemason.

I was surprised to find such impressive carvings and detailing of such quality, especially in the design of doors and entrances. For example at 41 Hailgate there are fluted columns and an impressive Doric pedimented porch. At 100-102 Hailgate (the town's longest and most winding street) the doors have delightful fanlights. And there is more to seek out at Howden Hall with its Westmorland slate roof, originally a manor house in Flatgate by glimpsing through a wrought-iron gate in the garden wall. One finds another Tuscan porch at Pinfold Street whith some of the best examples of rococo-like pediments at 36 Bridgegate and a wonderful, ebullient early nineteenth-century scroll and acanthus leaf decoration at 1 Vicar Lane. One of the Victorian shops shares the same rococo-ish exuberance and the diverse townscape flourishes in Bridgegate with its painted facades. Merchants, attorneys, surgeons and ministers were certainly house-proud in the external sense, had travelled and were influenced doubtless by what was happening in York. The possibilities of decoration in brick are exploited beyond measure and any lack of colour is redressed in the exceptionally fine fanlights and arches. Purpose-built Victorian shop fronts survive in the Market Place with two shops dating from the early nineteenth century having vast sash windows albeit with modest facades.

Number 2 Churchside, by the minster, is Jane Small's large Victorian house which has the look of an Italian merchant's property, but a nineteenth-century version, impressive and out of scale with its neighbouring houses. The grandeur puzzles me; there are three bays on the ground floor faced in stone and emphasised with Corinthian columns, with a prominent frieze above a bold cornice. Where had Miss Small been, I wondered? And where did she fit in the social and economic hierarchy of Howden?

Continuing along Churchside I found another larger market place where three pubs served the traders and merchants stood selling their sacks of corn in front of the west door of the minster. One has inset decorative corner turrets and contrasting red and black tiles, a hint of the Gothic revival style. I would describe Howden as brimful of character vernacular architecture. However, within a space of a few months, I saw some signs of creeping standardisation; the quite delightful post office with its charming green and white painted windows and robust lettering above had been treated to a pot of bureaucratic battleship grey. But all was well with the tiled front of the butcher's shop with its stocky lettering, decorated with Swaledale sheep. Another detail worth searching out is a small blue plaque let into the curved end of Hailgate, a narrow cobbled street barely wide enough for a small carriage but wide enough for a horse. Apart from the war memorial in the Market Place, built in 1920, there is little later than 1870. This is the period of the fine Shire Hall built in that year, which is more Hanseatic cloth hall style than Yorkshire; although of red brick it has a stepped gable and fish scale roof telling us that Howden's situation was still buoyant and looking eastward to its foreign buyers.

The town is well endowed with religious architecture, but the minster predominates the skyline. This was the centre of a vast foundation, once owned by the Prince Bishops of Durham and one of the largest churches in the East Riding. It was perfectly situated on the journey from London to Durham for refreshment of the Bishops staying at the Manor House. This has been recently restored, but is not open. The church once belonged to the Saxon monks of Peterborough Abbey and Roger de Hoveden was an early incumbent in 1174, and important chronicler of English history, continuing the work of Bede. He was esteemed for his fidelity and diligence and was a famous authority who flourished in Henry II's reign.

The minster became a collegiate church in 1267 when it acquired the decorated nave, replacing the earlier Norman one.

However, the octagonal chapter house which is now in ruins was the last to be built in England, possibly in 1380. Bishop Skirlaw provided funds for its building here, just as he did at York. It is worth trying to imagine just what a marvellous place of worship this church must have been in the fourteenth century. As a collegiate church it survived the dissolution of the monasteries, only to suffer when collegiate churches and chantries were in their turn dissolved in 1548. It was recorded as a church in the Domesday Book and the building plots several styles: English Decorated in the lavish nave completed in the early fourteenth century; the gorgeous carved stone pulpitum, with a splendid decorated fifteenth-century ogee arch, with fourteenth century sculpture in the niches. And a twentieth-century window inserted in 1953 portrays Howden's past luminaries. The chapter house, with a ledger stone by Eric Gill, and the ruined choir are now cut off from the nave.

My confidant invited me to see the chantries and statuary, giving me snippets of local history while local ladies decorated for the harvest festival with everything from potatoes – the best you can probably buy are found in the wolds – to flowers. Today the church is very much alive but there is no refectory, or a museum café, and the library on the ground floor of the Shire Hall was closed, but there are greengrocers, one run by the same lady and her husband for sixty years, and a cheese shop, and so I made the best of it.

I would have been delighted if tea had been served at the Shire Hall which once sat 500, even more so if I had found the sort of teas Winefred Holtby described in South Riding at the fictitious Floral Hall where the two shilling choice included crab sandwiches, the one and sixpence ham or potted meat with a fruit salad. Even the one shilling plain would have done me well with its cheesecakes, scones, spiced bread and currant tea cake. However, the exercise of decoding Howden's buildings was a treat in itself and I found some of the Yorkshire food I was seeking at Sledmere. I have a greedy joy in English dishes peculiar to their own region.

32

Kirkby Malham, Settle and Horton-in-Ribblesdale

North Yorkshire

The now famous Pennine Way was first dedicated at Kirkby Malham in the 1940s. Old customs, new pastimes and art are all blended here at St Michael's, dubbed the Cathedral of the Dales, which has inspired artists as Airedale has drawn poets. Wordsworth wrote of Malham Cove: 'No mightier work has gained the plausive smile;' it is said that Charles Kingsley wrote or gained the idea for The Water Babies here and Turner painted it. The dale continues to inspire such artists as the sculptor Judith Bluck, Joan Hassall, the engraver, and Bill Wild both drawing on the wildlife.

A delicate wrought-iron gate with fish worked in as part of the decoration leads to a spacious nave and two side aisles of St Michael's which have intricately carved box pews; the pew on the left of the altar is at least six feet high, the other has been lowered. In the vestry I found a sight I had not seen before in a church: a small tray was set out with juices, tea and the wherewithal to make a hot drink for visitors or walkers. Even as long ago as 1892 H Speight wrote that this region was dependent on tourism, and it really is so today.

From here I took the high road to Settle which runs with the fells on the right then a gated single-track across Kirkby Fell, a road without buildings, just the odd lozenge sign for passing places, an ear-popping road 1000 feet high. Settle has a reasonable helping of antique and tea shops and is positioned comfortably within the fells and a central market square. The Shambles has an imported look more of the borders or Cotswolds; the seventeenth-century arcading is now filled in and with Victorian upper storeys added.

For me, as I suspect it will be for most visitors, the Folly is the building which fascinates most. Although it is called the Folly I doubt it was built as one. The style is a mixture of Gothic and Renaissance, conjoining quite wittily. There is a scheme to make the Folly into a museum or heritage centre; in whatever capacity it is shown I just hope that it is opened up, as soon as funding will permit. I am curious about it. Most unusually the windows are of the wrap-around variety that we see so often on thirties housing, bypass mode, which derived from the Bauhaus movement. But this is of the seventeenth century. The corner is, therefore, a window post, not in stone, but in wood. The windows carry around the left side of the first floor, and so on at the right wing. One should examine the different levels: on the ground floor there is a run of wooden frames with Gothic arches in each section, on the first floor is the seventeenth-century moderne feature and in the central bay there is an arch on the second floor which alters the repeating pattern. The windows are rectangular with hood moulds, dropping like curtain tops. Neither Whitaker who wrote about this, or Pevsner have attributed this absorbing house to any one influence. I consider that it is the result of a travelled gentleman with a mind and eye of his own. The hand-out given by the tourist information centre suggests that Sir Richard Preston was up to the minute and open minded, as well as respecting of tradition.

The two unusual columns on either side of the main entrance suggest German influence. Franconians, it appears, worked in the lead mines, or did perhaps Flemish weavers even venture this far? Who knows? This is a puzzle awaiting a solution. I long to see the staircase and fireplaces. I made an architectural or artistic link with this building. Nikolaus Pevsner, who lectured in art history at Birkbeck College in London, and Dr Birkbeck, who was born in Settle, has a living legacy not just at London University, but everywhere where art appreciation courses are held under the auspices of the Workers Education Association. It was he who also founded the Institution of Mechanical Engineers.

The road from Settle, up through Ribblesdale, is a cyclist's and walker's paradise as the road widens out and rolls along the bottom of Pen-y-Ghent. This is one of three peaks whose climbing is rewarded by a medal or badge and tie. The Pen-y-Ghent café, situated on the now famous Pennine Way, makes no pretension to anything other than what it does naturally. It services the walkers and cyclists. Red formica tables, circa early 1960s, and serviceable wooden benches with a well stocked shop selling clothes, books, safety equipment and loads of maps greet you.

The Bayes family are a veritable encyclopedia of information on where to stay, where to eat and, of course walking. Cyclists and walkers are welcomed in whatever apparel they arrive in.

This is honest value and spotless.

While I was there, thinking about the walk but without the energy to do it, two Max Wall look-a-like cyclists came in with their turned up shoes and spindly thin lycra-clad legs on their Friday off. This is a break for the walking weary and the saddle-sore riders who can take time off to quaff tea in mugs and eat toasted sandwiches and tea cakes toasted with dripping butter. The food is the variety you do not have to think about: sausages, imported Chorley cakes (from Lancashire), Wensleydale cheese good homemade apple cake and of course, bacon sandwiches. Serious walkers, not the smart and colour-coordinated sort, but really serious walkers, walk on this.

The unique difference between the Pen-y-Ghent café and any of the other supporting tea rooms in this book is that this one also provides a safety service or a clocking-in system for walkers setting off on the Three Peaks marathon. A tea room which is a complete one-off that Wainwright would have appreciated, with the unpretentiousness of a pit stop, even though he could not have predicted or may not have approved of the Pennine Way industry, for which he sowed the seeds in the 1930s. I yearn to go back and walk in this dale with its spinneys further up and see more of the extraordinary viaducts.

The peak of Pen-y-Ghent towers above like a large sugar loaf, with Whernside and Ingleborough making the three. Wainwright's fells above Settle when he first made this walk in 1939 are the same: of soft grass 'velvety cropped close by sheep' where the limestone was 'gleaming white patches of stone, studding the fell sides like drifts of snow that have defied the sun.'

33

Parcevall Hall Gardens, Skyreholme

North Yorkshire

The hidden corners of England always amaze me; some are magical. Parcevall Hall Gardens qualifies on both accounts. On one of those blissful late April afternoons when the light is as clear as a bell I found what I can best describe as an almost secret garden, alone but not lonely, with sounds and extraordinary views. I like to imagine that Charlotte Brontë visited this spot. The gardens may have given a different picture, but the sequestered peace and isolation would not have changed.

Why is it so distinctive? From wherever you stand, on the terraces at the peak of the cliff walk, among the orchards or woodland, this is a serene experience. The position, of course, spreading upwards from a valley, harmonises yet contrasts with the rock top of Simon's Seat. The combination of orchards and terraces, the ascent and descent, the hues and, above all, stillness are the essence of Parcevall Hall. The stillness comes from the seclusion of the garden and, I suspect, from the house now used as a retreat under the auspices of Walsingham. Whether on foot or in a car the arrival is sudden and unexpected, as the gardens, set in the valley, almost appear to have been dropped into the landscape, between fells with the road to Greenhow and the serious part of the Pennine chain.

Missing the turning to Skyreholme, as I did, is no bad thing; it allows you to see the whole panorama and relationship to the fells from the road above. Skyreholme was in the Manor of Appletreewick, belonging to Bolton Priory before the Dissolution. But in spite of its name it is more famous for onions than apples. This has been remedied by the large apple-planting programme at Parcevall and there are enough varieties now in the gardens to justify the name. Through Skyreholme, on a very sharp turn, there are unusual three-storey cottages where paper mill workers once lived, and the road leads to the Hall which is not open. A steep drive takes you on and past the house to the centre of the gardens.

It was only in 1927 that the gardens were recovered and

restored in harmony with the region and its geology. The key to this are the stones and rubble which were used from a demolished barn to build the terraces below the house, now offering a private view of the moors. Even with a considerable labour force it took thirty years to complete the gardens. Although man's signature is written fairly large, it is a sensitive script. It should not be forgotten that the pastimes and pleasures of the rich landowners have left the landscape as it is today and the Bolton estate is very much man-moulded: grouse shoots need extensive moors and even the monks had their stew ponds.

The garden follows a triangular shape with Tarn Ghyll beck at the bottom, fanning out from the entrance with the cliff garden at the top, or the apex dropping down through the orchards as the site widens to a rock garden, terraces and chapel garden. Terraces are placed to take advantage of an amazing vista. These are processional, leading down and drawing again to the opposite fell of Simon's Seat. The gardens' success is dependent on the soil type; some areas are a mix of millstone grit and lime, thus encouraging the growth of many species of rhododendron. Before the woodland planting, St Cuthbert's Wood, now with blue cedar, western red cedar, viburnum and camellias was begun, the whole area was covered in barren hill pasture.

The rhododendrons, orchards, rare shrubs, and other planting are designed to give continuous colour and perfume through the year: scarlet willows with their bright red branches in winter, hamamelis with its spiky flowers filling the air with wonderful scent in February and March. The rhododendrons' palette runs from rose pink to deep red and yellow. The white-scented late-flowering species was a favourite of Sir William Milner who bought the property in 1927 and planned the garden. In April the grass under the orchards looked as though someone had taken a paint brush dripping with shades of yellow and swathed the ground below the old-fashioned varieties of apple, varieties that you hardly ever see, and are even less likely to taste unless you come here. Varieties which endure the northern climes have been specially selected. Among the long list are names which roll off the tongue: Ribston Pippin, Newton Wonder, Gasgoigne's Scarlet, Yorkshire Greening, King of Pippins, Yorkshire beauty and Ashmead Kernal, which makes a good juice. Have you ever come across an apple called Gooseberry? It is here. The pears: Knights' Monarch, William Bon Chretien, Windsor, and, of course, the crab apples. I hope the tea room will make their own version of this amber coloured jelly and serve it for tea.

The daffodil bank on the south-west side glows with the colours of thousands of plants: yellow, primrose and parchment-coloured, pheasant eye and home-raised seedlings overlooking the old kitchen gardens which have been ploughed up. A different mood springs from the terraces, another area of seclusion with the sound of running water. The colours of the primulas in the outer courtyard ran the whole gamut of pink. This is one of the most exciting planned gateways looking towards the fell top of Simon's Seat. (This has its own legend: a shepherd found a baby boy on the rocks which he and other village shepherds saved and brought up as their own.)

Climbing plants cloth the grey stone of the seventeenth-century house on the terrace: Albertine rose, laburnum and lilac all take their turn to show their best colours and perfume this part of the garden where a crinodendron bears its hanging crimson blossom in May. The beds are full of primroses, wallflowers and ceanothus.

Only three gardeners, who always seem to have a new scheme up their sleeves, tend and plan this sanctuary of a garden. And now the trustees have opened a tea room in what was the gardener's house. One would expect no less dedication to the art of

Yorkshire baking than that given to gardening. The guide book has been written for aficionados; they write that they hope the visitors will be refreshed and strengthened. There is little doubt of this.

34

Shandy Hall and Coxwold village

North Yorkshire

Shandy Hall is no mere house, but the former home and memorial to Laurence Sterne who wrote the nine small volumes of Tristram Shandy. Shandy Hall positively glows, it contains the Sterne collection of Mr and Mrs Monkman who, with others, set up a charitable trust in order to save and preserve the home of one of England's most famous novelists.

The newly famous Sterne became parson to the parish of Coxwold in 1760. Soon the Parsonage House became known as Shandy Hall. Shandy was an old dialect name for odd, and he appropriated it for the name of his hero Tristram Shandy. His fans and visitors to this house, his 'philosophical hut', will be as fascinated as I was by Sterne's own improvements, the contemporary prints and the profusion of Shandeana. His writing spawned a whole industry of souvenirs and knick-knacks, of glass, cartoons, and ceramics equal to, or maybe the precedent of, the twentieth-century idol T-shirt.

What the Monkmans visited in 1963 a distressed, medieval, fifteenth-century house with rotting timbers, is now a home where every wooden surface is polished, loved and cared for. Today's garden is a small paradise where it was once a jungle. It was a privilege to walk around the house and talk to the Monkmans, the honorary curators. After several attempts to visit Shandy Hall, I realised why the visits are carefully managed on just two opening days a week in summer. The very personal tour would not be possible with more people.

The tour starts in the kitchen, a warm room, furnished with Windsor chairs and a buffed York stone floor, leading off the garden where I was invited to sit and appreciate the warm hub of the house which has a friendly and familiar feel. Here, Mrs Monkman explained the original condition, although the house has become a means of showing their collection. A rather tall, early nineteenth-century fireplace dominates but does not obscure the remains of the earlier medieval or hall house. But there are some earlier details, such as an eighteenth-century fitted shelf or half-dresser with an interesting pot board.

The study is next to the kitchen, only nine foot square but perfectly formed, with books on three sides, a window on to the village and an Adam fireplace. Although the guide tells us that Sterne was untidy, there is little evidence today for this is neat and crisp. An entrancing space. Who would not wish to write here? As Sterne wrote: 'I am as happy as a prince at Coxwold.' But even Sterne had his 'blocks'; he counteracted these by changing his clothes and putting on a better wig, or coat, or a favourite ring, and thus redressed, or refreshed he wrote: 'a man cannot dress, but his ideas get cloth'd at the same time.'

The dining room is on a pleasant scale with low ceilings and original door handles with panels painted in soothing Adam green on which the contemporary cartoons, taken from Tristam Shandy, a Sentimental Journey, hang. A large glass cabinet displays first editions of the book, from worldwide translations to a reassuring orange and white banded pre-war Penguin books edition. In the double-aspect drawing room Sterne's alterations and improvements are bold. He contrived to embrace the garden by adding a small wing nearest the exterior, pulling both landscape and light inwards. As elsewhere, a highly informed guide showed us the panel covering a large medieval wall painting which may reinforce the links with nearby Newburgh Priory. There is just one piece of furniture which has been traced directly to Sterne; this is a twenty-inch square table with small elegant drop handles.

Lastly I collected myself in the pale geranium garden room, part of the Sterne's extension, before going back and seeing the whole again. Shandy Hall more than justifies that hackneyed term – unique. The essence of the past, the writer, his room, the guides and the position are a pleasure to savour, and there is the garden. This has an arcaded terrace with the whole length taken up by a seat which Sterne called 'a sweet Pavilion', with lawns beyond. Each small arch frames a different aspect – a walled garden, a profusion of clematis, mowed paths, shrubs and cow parsley in what is designed to be semi-cultivated wilderness. In the Quarry garden wild flowers are left to do as they wish. Aqualigea, phlox, honesty, a bank covered with comfrey and a garden seat connects between the house and garden. There are Welsh poppies, alchemilla, cat mint full of bees and blooms of Canterbury bells leaning off one wall, mingling with daisies and a marvellous variegated elder. This is all soft, there is nothing angular, a neat house and garden with many moods. At the end are the fields, with sheep and hills beyond. The Shandy shop, or bothy, sells energy-giving comb honey and there are home-reared plants for sale with cordon fruit growing nearby. Tristam's father was much concerned with the development of 'wall fruit' and his green-gages, which in September were ready for pulling.

Coxwold has a very wide street similar to Burford in Oxfordshire, with gorgeous vernacular architecture. The almshouses of 1660 were given by Lord Fauconberg, Sterne's patron; there is a rare thatched pub and a handful of gentle-men's houses. The church is another St Michael's and All Angels (churches were named after St Michael when they were built on the site of early pagan temples). Records show that this was one of three minsters that had to be repaired with Ripon and Fountains by King Eadbert of Northumbria in 757. The struc-ture, however, is principally fifteenth century and Sterne only had to cross the road to preach in it.

At the bottom of the village street a tea room in the old school house, with pretty fret-work porch does as the sign says and serves 'high teas' of ham and eggs, salad and good cakes, in the garden outside. In the opposite lane the Coxwold Pottery, whose charming studio and courtyard display area with more herbs and honey, has been built of reclaimed doors and windows from a railway station. The work has a green flowing naturalistic character. I was told that visitors still remember coming here to Coxwold to enjoy the village by train on excursions just after the First World War. Coxwold's joy is that it is still all of a piece, in Edmund Vale's words; 'it is a thing which has become beautiful, without design or art, merely because it has gone on and on being the place where every kind of thing has happened at one time or another'. The continuity of a village pulls at the heart-strings, if just one constituent goes, the shop or the post office, it begins to bleed.

From Coxwold to Danby I went through and past a host of beautiful situations. For a moment or two I stopped to look at the

ruins of Byland Abbey, to which Sterne walked and I stopped at Helmsley, with its wonderful square and the Crown pub whose high tea finishes at 5.45pm and I have not yet arrived in time! One travels up and over Sutton Bank, the edge of the North Yorkshire moors. I stopped in the evening to look again at Rievaulx Abbey; the contrast between Reivaulx and Byland is sharp. The latter is set right down on a corner bend flat on a field, while the former lies in a valley, deep down like Fountains, with the beech and rowan trees of Sutton Bank making it one of the most romantically placed abbeys.

35

Skipton

North Yorkshire

Skipton is as Skipton does. Charming Skipton, with an informal mixture of the remains of manufacturing and Picturesque manages to combine its everyday, market town getting-on-with-life attitude, with its famed castle, and position as a gateway to the beautiful Dales.

Skipton is also resilient; it withstood two sieges during the Wars of the Roses and in the Civil War. But the castle, whose refurbishment was directed by Lady Anne Clifford in 1658, is very much part of the town, along with the church. The castle was built by the Romille family in 1090 on rock, with fine views to the south and the natural defence of the cliff face to the north and the Eller Beck below. Lady Anne was as important to seventeenth-century Skipton as the church and castle are to the town today. Both stand at the top of a wide, gently sloping market street looking over to the fells.

The first sight is the two large round towers which lead through the arch via the site of a concealed drawbridge on the town side. After the gatehouse another seven towers of the main buildings face into the inner bailey. These architectural towers of strength remain Skipton's character. One of the most conspicuous but less hostile decorative details, added by Lady Anne, is the carving Desormais (meaning henceforth) let into the balustrade between the two main gate towers. This is one of England's best preserved castles and has a partially restored chapel. The castle is shown in a manner reflecting its original important military purpose and it is still Lady Anne's key which is used to lock the huge oak doors of the main gate each evening.

Lady Anne was a royalist and politically astute; her careful restoration was designed not to antagonise parliament so the original towers were not restored to their original fortifying height. But she recreated the medieval features, repairing the kitchen and the great hall, using lead mined at Grassington. When here, during in the Commonwealth, she stayed in the octagonal tower not far from the Barden estates and organised

129

beating of the bounds to confirm her inheritance in 1651. The Renaissance grotto made by Lady Anne's cousin Henry, the fifth Earl – the only other is at Woburn (Lady Anne's mother was a Russell) – is quite spectacular, a room with walls encrusted with shells, a rare creation of the seventeenth century.

The most evocative space in the well-designed tour of the rooms that are open to the public is the conduit courtyard where Lady Anne planted the yew and where her initials are formed in the top of the lead pipework. This is one of the finest spaces I have seen for absorbing and imagining the daily comings and goings of a sixteenth and seventeenth-century noble family and their servants. This court was built by Henry the Shepherd Lord to live in after the Wars of the Roses, a softer more domestic contrast to the castle and a reaction to the disastrous family losses. The court provided the water for the castle, and from it there are several doorways, steps and the windows of the new kitchen which was converted in the 1680s by the Earl of Thanet, the owner through the marriage of the second Earl to Lady Anne's eldest daughter Margaret. (The older medieval kitchen is on the first floor of the twelfth-century castle.) Also looking into the courtyard is the curing room with its elegant stone sink under the window where meat was salted and cured ready for the winter. This is a rare chance for visitors to have such an intimate relationship with a building, its owners and its different building styles. The Tudor wing with its mullioned windows built by the Shepherd Lord's grandson, the second Earl, on his marriage to the niece of Henry VIII, Lady Eleanor Brandon.

Today's owners take equal pride in the ongoing care and restoration without unwelcome twentieth-century inclusions. Skipton is overflowing with historical connections. I found a more recent one between Skipton, Cumberland and Heelis the solicitors (Beatrix Potter married Mr Heelis in the 1920s). It appears that Heelis were the agents for the Earl of Thanet when Whitaker was writing his History of Craven in the nineteenth-century, and gave him permission to inspect the muniments room in the castle.

Lady Anne was born here in 1590 on January 30. Her father, Lord Cumberland, who championed Queen Elizabeth and fought in the Armada, is buried in the parish church where Lady Anne was christened. The family to whom Charlotte Brontë was governess are also buried here. This church, a parish church in the truest sense of the word, is at the very heart of the community. In the ever-filled vestry room many local groups meet, from the WI to the children's dance classes and a café, called the Honeypot, on Fridays. The ministry of welcome is immediate.

Food is served on Friday and Saturday, being two of the four market days, overseen by Dzidra Butterfield, the daughter of a Latvian émigré married to a Yorkshire man. She is dedicated to organic produce and makes her gargantuan scones (only on Friday) with Doves Farm flour. This café tries to be all things as far as possible to everyone, so that the character of the food changes from Friday to Saturday and the little café has to change its clothes quickly, reverting back to meeting room or activity room when needed.

The spirit of giving and sharing predominates; where possible Dzidra uses donations, rhubarb, for example, for their excellent crumble. She makes thick soups in winter: mushroom and barley, leek and potato, the stuff of the Dales. With a good crew of volunteers, she oversees the baking of favourite sponges, coffee, chocolate and victoria, and makes Yorkshire fat rascals and the farmhouse treat, a large rock cake made with honey which fills up shoppers and walkers. Salad ingredients are home-grown or organic and the café, with its own green data base of suppliers and goods in Skipton, is part of the church ecology group. The prime ingredient of the ploughman's lunches could be cheese from Derek Priestley's stall just across in the market; you can taste other local farm cheeses: Coverdale, Wensleydale or Ribblesdale here.

Yet advertisements are placed in the parish magazine in the hope that friends will bring surplus herbs, salads, fruit and vegetables. They could even make a salmangundi, an English salad, if there were a chicken and herrings, which with produce from their kitchen gardens would make a lovely set piece salad. Chutneys, relishes and jams, gooseberry and orange, and redcurrant jelly, are also made with fruit gifts. I tasted the first arrival of the raspberry jam which was almost intoxicating. On Saturdays the menu is described as more homely and traditional for the marketeers when 'you can hardly get a seat'. The Saturday salmon and cucumber tart would grace any table, the carrot cake was carroty and the victoria sponge light. Some of the dishes I research yet rarely encounter on counters, such as ground rice tarts, meat stews and pies, are served.

The circle of good English food at Skipton was squared when I discovered that Dorothy Hartley had included the kitchen at the convent and the food she cooked at Skipton, in her seminal work Food in England, and indeed The Craven Heifer Inn and its tea, in the early decades of this century. This was real hefty Yorkshire tea of ham, tea cakes, honey, conserves, black treacle and game pies and apple pies.

Holy Trinity stands facing the length of the High Street and market. The stalls embroider either side of the street, with shapes, colour and noise. In the fourteenth century Skipton was a commercial centre for wool, weaving and spinning and there are still plenty of good terraced houses and old shop fronts with many courts and alleys, showing the burgage plots and mills running down to the beck.

This church was founded with the help of the Bolton Abbey monks who came here in the thirteenth century. It replaced an earlier wooden church and is Perpendicular, that is English in style, with thin buttresses and a pinnacled tower. Like so many of the Wharfedale churches the nave has an exterior crenellated roof line. There are examples of each century's gifts and fashions in the interior. The sedilia in the south aisle, with four carved seats where priests would sit, is fourteenth-century, the decorated bosses carved in the beams are of the same period, there is a seventeenth-century Jacobean revolving font cover and a high Tudor decorated wooden oak screen, perhaps originally painted, as the beams and rafters of the sixteenth century were also treated. Holy Trinity was also attacked in the Civil War, suffered a fire in the tower in the nineteenth century, and as recently as the 1920s another fire in the organ. But it has benefited from gifts, not only from Lady Anne but it is believed from Richard III, Duke of York, whose castle was at Middleham in Wensleydale.

The Craven Museum resides above the town hall, built in 1862 classical style with a pedimented portico on the upper floor.

Here is a treasure trove of material objects which fill in the jigsaw of history. Display cases are jam-packed with exhibits and fragments, under glass and at the right height. Within a limited space they host temporary travelling exhibitions. The unusual artefacts include an Iron Age stone head, so old and so smooth he could almost be contemporary, the accoutrements of lead mining: the miner's soft hat held hard with glue and his tiny brass lamp. And of course many farming objects: the more gruesome side of husbandry such as tail-docking implements, or an illustration of the Craven heifer, bred on the Bolton estate. This extraordinarily large beast was taken by its owner as a touring exhibit to fairs until he lost it in a wager.

Skipton became even more of a meeting point for trade in 1774 when the Leeds to Liverpool canal was finished, enabling it to trade in wood as well as textiles, lead from the nearby mines, lime and limestone which was once quarried vigorously. The town has some older shop fronts: Nelson's is from the 1920s, a shoe shop with strong angular deco script in pale aqua on a black vitrolite, and the art nouveau windows at the Craven Herald bookshop. But the 'huckster ribbon and thread stalls' that you see here in the market, an early one founded in 1204, are the descendants of the old packmen who went from farm to farm, and the trade descends from the farmers who came to market, to gossip, to eat their dinner and sell their beasts. The market is now held at a new and neater auction mart just outside the town where, I am told, there are performances of Shakespeare in the open. So Skipton still provides drama among the scents and the country sounds of the land as it did 300 years ago.

36

Sledmere House and Sledmere village

East Yorkshire

Sledmere House appears Georgian but is in fact an Edwardian replacement of an eighteenth-century house, burnt down in 1911, where quite miraculously the contents were saved. The Georgian house was established in 1751 by Richard Sykes, High Sheriff of York, on an earlier medieval site in a square plan. His nephew, Sir Christopher Sykes, who inherited in 1783, enlarged and added two wings which gave greater importance and movement to the facade. He also faced the house in Nottingham stone and changed the focus of the main approach towards the south. Sledmere is significant for it is associated with three important eighteenth-century designers, John Carr as the architect, Joseph Rose for the decorative plaster work and Capability Brown for the gardens.

The house has a controlled appearance with an elegant design in a vertical H-plan. Its purpose was to house Sir Christopher's collection and provide a family home fitting his position as a patron of the arts. Sir Christopher kept a close eye on the improvements, consulting Samuel Wyatt and John Carr, who designed the Deer House and the castle, both follies and some of the farm buildings. The commissioning of Joseph Rose was important as he had worked with Robert Adam, from whom he must have assimilated ideas such as Adam's technique of designing niches in the entrance hall for showing statuary, which Adam first used at Newby Hall.

After the fire each room, as far as possible, was reconstructed by Walter Brierley, a York architect called the Edwin Lutyens of Yorkshire. He used Rose's original drawings and referred to watercolours for the interiors; amazingly, the original moulds were discovered at a works in London. The entrance hall has great poise with columns, frieze and plasterwork. The pale biscuit stone floor, with inlaid bands of green Roche stone recovered from Roche Abbey, contributes to this elegance. The progression through the hall to the wide graceful double staircase with round-edged treads at the base is an exercise worth repeating. Every room gives a good view of the far-reaching gardens.

Sir Christopher, who is accompanied by his wife in a portrait by George Romney which hangs in the dining room, accumulated his library on the Grand Tour. He bought a rare edition of the Gutenberg Bible in two volumes; a great part of the collection had to be sold in the nineteenth century to counteract the crippling effects on agriculture of the Napoleonic wars, but the collection had been as famous as those at Longleat and Chatsworth. With a fine sense of space the design and setting conveys intimacy: for here the family used to gather with each member taking up his chosen occupation. The relationship to the gardens is perfect and as the room spans the width of the south front you can see the landscape which is transported nearer with the two follies, the temple-like Deerhouse with strict Tuscan columns and the castle, which reflect the Georgian love affair with the Gothick and Romantic. One can see other examples of the fashion for nineteenth-century Gothic or medieval revival in the village where Sir Christopher moved the original community because it obscured his view.

In this rich library I was permitted to handle a receipt book on vellum of 1679, with one page written in Arabic, yet to be translated. I found whipped possets and plum cakes with caraway seeds, hartshorn jelly and a wonderful-sounding raspberry cake. The last is simply undiluted raspberries and sugar reduced to what I would describe as a fruit cheese, set on a plate and cut. I would like to think that some of these will be developed for visitors to Sledmere.

Owners of country houses have always commissioned fine art and furniture, and that tradition continues with pieces of contemporary work at Sledmere. One bedroom has furniture by David Linley who designed a dressing table, occasional table and stool in walnut, inlaid with ebony, ash and sycamore. This complements the striking bed made on the estate in the early twentieth century in mahogany with walnut, sycamore and ash. In the church one finds new stained-glass work and modern stone carving.

Sledmere has a sense of being lived in; the organ is played on open days in the hall, making one feel like a guest, the house is immaculate, fresh flowers fill the rooms and the staff all belong, relishing the chance to answer questions and eager to share information and anecdotes. Sledmere positively welcomes its visitors and their interest; viewing is not rationed.

The village may have been moved but there is an impressive 250 years' worth of architectural styles and fashions, the work of several esteemed Victorian architects. The church was designed by Temple Moore and a row of cottages by G E Street. The eighteenth-century shop has a charming double window, a pantile roof almost an artwork in brick; the oldest surviving Triton cottage dates from 1700. Another group of houses in the Tudor revival style in cheerful red brick housing the post office and clerk's house was designed by John Birch and is part of the patronage of Sir Tatton Sykes, the fifth baronet, together with the school and schoolmaster's house. And the patronage continued with twelve neo-Georgian estate houses built in 1946, designed by Jack Gold, with some of the material that was demolished by Brierly from the service wing.

Anyone who has visited other stud farms or villages will recognise the comfortable relationship of farm and estate cottages. At Sledmere these are picked out in the cream and maroon paint; brick walls surround the house. Brick looks best in this landscape. From these stables Sir Tatton Sykes, the fourth baronet, bred Derby, Oaks and St Leger winners, and he rode from Sledmere down to Epsom for the Derby. The bloodstock connection is reinforced with the fine paintings by Ferneley and Herring in the Horse Room, inside the house, while in the yellow brick stables, possibly by Carr, an exhibition space celebrates the work of the Sykes family who built, improved and donated so much in the county.

The tea room is also in the stable wing and has the sort of gossip-laden atmosphere that is manufactured by serious tea takers who think nothing of driving thirty miles to indulge their habit. My tea was excellent, with a large piece of Yorkshire tea bread and a very generous slice of Wensleydale. Happily, this menu offers sustaining dishes of the type once served for high tea until five o'clock, such as fisherman's pie and smoked haddock rarebit. Roast beef and Yorkshire pudding are popular lunchtime dishes; with bread and butter pudding. The soup might be red lentil or leek and potato, served in the autumn when pheasant casserole or pork chops arrive with apple chutney. Home-baked light scones, parkin, apricot and almond, or lemon and coconut sponges, as well as date and oatmeal cake are served for tea.

Here I found the names that spell out a regional food heritage. We could realistically add Yorkshire turf cakes, with the equine connection, or even fat rascals. The rather modest service area does not detract, nonetheless I felt one strand of elegance could be allowed to cross from the house without incorporating pastiche.

In Winefred Holtby's South Riding, set in this area, the tea table for a council member 'waited, silver kettle bubbling and shining teapot already warmed, caddy of Earl Grey mixture, a covered plate of buttered anchovy toast, and angel cake like a sugar snowdrift...silver without finger marks, cloth without crease'. Perhaps this is set out today for house guests by the efficient and experienced butler, who so kindly showed me the receipt book. The dedicated staff are proud of working for a family who took care of them. For example, in 1879, upwards of 200 tenants and their dependants were entertained in the library, laid out like one vast dining room. On the other hand the meanness of Christopher Sykes' eccentric and lovable great-aunt Venetia was used in all kinds of ways to reduce the household bills. She may have been a society hostess married to a wealthy American, Arthur James, entertaining and being entertained by the royal family, yet these extraordinary ruses would surely have saved pennies, not pounds. She ordered meat on sale or return for her parties in London, returning the joint on Monday if it were uneaten. Leftovers were used in every imaginable dish; then she discovered that by inviting as many Roman Catholics as possible to Friday dinners she could serve fish and save on the meat bill. At one party staff were ordered to make one single chicken serve ten, no mean feat, through a coded message – D C S C – handed to the butler: 'Do not cut the second chicken.'

But today for a visitor the line in Christopher Sykes' book The Visitor epitomises Sledmere: 'The air at Sledmere is deliciously sweet compared with London's restless days and languid nights – a calm inaccessible refuge.'

37

Swaledale

North Yorkshire

On the longest day of the year, having started out from Dunstanburgh in Northumberland, I took a winding and diverting journey, stopping at Rowlands Gill, Hexham, Stocksfield and Cherryburn (a must for Thomas Bewick fans), through sandstone Staindrop and onwards to Barnard Castle, Kirkby Stephen and the beginning of Swaledale.

This journey took me through a land of rivers: the Wear, the Derwent, the Tyne, the Tees and the Coquet, to the Bowes Museum, a museum to approach in the evening, one of the most unexpected sites in the North at Barnard Castle, more like an architectural fugitive from the Loire. See the collection, it is unforgettable and of national importance. Barnard Castle connects Northumberland, Cumbria and the Yorkshire Dales, facing east and west, the only town on the A66 through Cumbria, on a road which gives glimpses of the folds and an exciting panorama of dales below.

'Barny' is a place that has seen better days and needs some money injecting into some of its excellent buildings. It sits on a steep hill with a border town feel and gritstone houses of character, cobbled streets with a wide old market place. Next, Kirkby Stephen, which is smaller but no less agreeable with some fine buildings: an exceptional Arts and Crafts-style Martins Bank, alleyways and cobbled corners, medieval backs, a butter market, and a sandstone fourteenth-century church. There is a stunning Temperance Hall of 1856. It is a town that must have prospered from knitting.

This was my circuitous route to the middle of Swaledale and Gunnerside, where I stayed. Swaledale is perhaps one of the last romantic journeys that can be taken on a made-up road which heavy traffic will never be allowed to spoil. From west to the east at Reeth or Richmond, it is, an enchanted excursion for Midsummer's Eve which will be for ever imprinted in my memory. The climb starts at the western head just out of Kirkby Stephen where the road begins its twenty-mile sweep, and a sign:

'last fill up for 20 miles.' Around a bend, beyond the town, the change to moor is instant. Immediately I was in another world – that of Swaledale. At once there were drystone walls, and at last I saw the Swaledale sheep in their home land. This is second-gear terrain, and stopping to take the first pictures I was surrounded by a chorus of curlews with their long beaks, flying past like heavily laden Wellington bombers. Heaven, just heaven. The horizon fluctuated with swatches of every shade in the green palette; lime green and yellow green, shades turning before me with the setting sun behind. For the first five or so miles I did not see or hear anything other than bleating new lambs, the crying curlews and the murmuring Swale which swung back and forth, sometimes converging with the road.

No one lives in the first stretch of rough moorland where my favourite stone walling, in the Yorkshire idiom, is as prolific as anywhere else, some with sharp through stones for strength – a complete contrast to Northumberland and Cumbria, where I had been earlier – others with two rows of through stones, one almost at the top below the top stone and the other a foot or so lower. Yet another had three rows of through stones. Why? For winter protection?

After the first steep climb the road drops down to a one in seven incline out of the moorland into the patchwork of barn country, punctated with limestone crags and with black cattle, grazing fields and the first signs of human habitation: the odd ruined barn, a tin shed, a telephone box and a tree! The road up to Tan Hill, not suitable for heavy vehicles, leads to the first house and Keld, the first village, which has a youth hostel. A further climb and then suddenly at least twenty field barns, one it seemed almost every few yards, in the flower-filled meadows, painted yellow, pink, blue, almost waist high. After Thwaite, it becomes less rugged, with more trees. Next is Muker (formerly spelt Mewachre), which is quite a centre. Its Victorian literary institute has a William and Mary style of gable end, a village shop and church. On that weekend they were commemorating the first centenary of a brass band playing to celebrate Queen Victoria's golden jubilee the day after midsummer in 1897.

The tea shop has a capacious teapot sign which hangs outside what was formerly the vicarage. Here you can buy local honey and cheese and hearty snacks of Yorkshire pudding, and their Yorkshire rarebit has a slice of gammon for good measure. Their own old peculiar fruit cake comes with a bonus slice of Swaledale cheese. In late May and early June many visitors arrange their holidays so that they coincide with the Muker Festival, and the Muker Show in early September is an event I hope to enjoy one day. As I was finishing this essay I heard that Prince Charles had visited Swaledale and had made a special request to have tea on the Terrace at Muker, the picture of him taking tea appeared in The Times the following weekend. Now I understood the tenacity of the farmers who endure such very hard winter conditions but for what reward, to live and be in the centre of such a vision.

But there are small signs of invasion and intrusiveness. Under the ESA scheme (Environmentally Sensitive Areas) farmers have to wait until an agreed European date before they can cut the flower meadows, not before the seed heads are ready. An odd world when farmers have to be told when to cut their hay in order to get a subsidy rather than a penalty. Surely they know. Another change in the landscape is the alien black lumps of plastic-covered hay that are no substitute for the haystacks or stoops and bales which were part of the landscape. These black mounds look intrusive, almost as though they were dropped from the sky. I cannot connect them with hay gathering, either in smell or sight.

I discovered that farmers from Swaledale went up to the Great Exhibition of 1851 to look at the displays but did not gain many new ideas; they had been, however, forward thinking in their agricultural policies in the eighteenth century when they planted ash and birch to restore the landscape, and today a policy of replanting the cropped tops continues. Like Pateley Bridge this was a lead mining area and like other Yorkshire dales villages there is a fine looking Wesleyan chapel.

The next village, Gunnerside, also has a literary institute, a pub, church and shop. And then as the valley widened out towards Reeth the hedges were full of dog roses and I noticed puffs of smoke coming from the chimneys even in high summer although it was light until 10.15pm above Gunnerside where I stayed. If you want to see lanes and meadows as you may not have seen before or for a long time, see Swaledale.

Reeth is one of the last villages before the end of the valley at Richmond where the river opens out to run down the next stages of a long journey to the Humber and the east coast. Reeth has a very large market green and a really exceptional bakery, unmissable with its loaf sign signifying homemade bread. Here the makings of a picnic can be bought for those with a pocket knife: fresh bread, Swaledale or Wensleydale cheese, homemade jams and curds, for which walkers and cyclists were queuing gratefully on a Sunday morning. Reeth has another literary institute built in 1850 and its own museum.

The museum is a good place to find out more of the way of life behind the landscape. Objects include a genuine sign for a ham and eggs tea, troughs and small presses for Wensleydale cheese. The standard of living was not high and in the nineteenth century the population was just slightly above what it was in 1580. Here is evidence of hand-knitting, brilliant socks and gloves. There are copper cheese kettles, tin cheese troughs, butter-making implements, the complete vocabulary of butter: horn cream skimmers, Scotch hands, butter churns and scales to weigh the finished product. The local WI must have commissioned its own china: its cups and saucers had a deep purple badge. The museum is very much part of the village but what I really enjoyed was seeing a living tradition taking place on the village green. The game of quoits is northern; there are or were Dales leagues. The player throws his quoit, an iron ring, next to a hob and a three-inch high peg. He then has to throw it from the platform where the hob is set in clay to the next hob. The quoit weighs five and a half pounds, the hob in its square yard of clay is another eleven yards distant. There are two running parallel which the players work their way up and down. The scoring is easy but it is a somewhat hazardous game where skill is needed. The pleasant ringing sound echoed across the green.

After Reeth the dale flattens out, the fields are hedge-edged and there is more livestock, and it becomes less rugged. Richmond makes a fitting end to this excursion. It is a fortified town with a magnificently sited Norman castle and one sheer-drop view down to the scurrying Swale. Richmond has one of the most romantic of market places, rising up to the higher ground, many of the streets are cobbled and steep. There are cheese and fish stalls in the market, a good grocer, a second-hand bookshop and not least a handful of elegant buildings which includes the oldest theatre in the country, an impressive military museum and some large successful-looking coaching inns. In one of the best buildings I accidentally came across the Saturday morning crowd of the town. The beautiful small town hall, with curving exterior steps, leaves its civic position and becomes the Saturday coffee room where varying groups and societies take it in turns to host the fray. Coffee and tea are brought to the table, the sound of conversation is harmonious, and wherever you sit you are bound to meet someone while the inside of the Georgian building, with its small council chamber and elegant windows, can be admired. Like Swaledale this is time out, but here time out socially, a real taste of a market town. What I really wanted to do was to turn around and go all the way to the head of the valley again.

38

The Nidderdale Museum, Pateley Bridge

North Yorkshire

The moor road from Parcevall Hall Gardens over Greenhow to Pateley Bridge disguises part of an industrial region which 100 years ago would have rung with the sounds of axe on stone. Lead was mined for thousands of years. The construction of the Gouthwaite reservoir gave employment to hundreds of men. At one stage two railways operated here, now there are none. Nidderdale is less an area of agricultural villages, more one of industrial hamlets.

The unprepossessing building in high Victorian style which houses the Nidderdale Museum was originally the Union Workhouse. In its own way the Nidderdale Museum is a large cabinet of curiosities, with each room unfolding and revealing its little treasures, and the corridor walls are avenues of local history and information. Not surprisingly this museum won a National Heritage award in 1990. Nidderdale is a collective collection, conceived by Nidderdale for Nidderdale, and for us 'up-cum-dens' who want to share.

First the workhouse: this was designed for both orphan and pauper, and though it was everyone's fear to fetch up in the poorhouse, one gathers from the menu displayed in the museum that inmates may well have eaten better than their town counterparts who were struggling with the depression in the last quarter of the nineteenth century. The food programme which indicates a somewhat sexist approach, gives precise portions and variations through the week. Bread and pea soup, suet pudding, six ounces of bread, one and a half pints of gruel for the men, who were also given half a pint of coffee, for some reason on a Friday, while women were given bread and butter and tea. The timetabling of hot drinks puzzles me; why coffee on Friday? Perhaps an end-of-week-bonus, but it was also served on two other days, with tea on another and cocoa on the remaining three. Nevertheless, there were reasonable amounts of fresh meat and vegetables.

The industrial and social history displays encompass the variety of this dale. Lead mining can be traced to the Brigantes, possibly before the Roman occupation. During the Middle Ages it was mined and sent via Aldborough across the Nidd to York and then on to London. The roof of Windsor Castle was covered with this lead in 1363. Farming was secondary because of the land's poor grit content. Scot Gate Ash quarry also provided stone for many famous buildings including the York barracks, York station and the three reservoirs built to support the large cities such as Bradford.

The Angram reservoir was finished in the First World War and the Scar in 1937. In 1921, with the construction of the Scar, several of the workers were housed in the Union. Others were spread between ten hotels, houses and bungalows. The reservoir was the single largest stone structure built in Europe and an extra railway was necessary for this project. A small town was built to house and support the workers with shops, schools, hotels, a canteen and even a cinema. Their facilities, running water and electricity, were probably more up to date than those of other workers living in Pateley Bridge.

Flax spinning was the other source of income. Gills Mill at Summerbridge, Glasshouse and Shaw Mills all spun and dressed flax on the hank and sold it to Knaresborough to be spun into cloth, although cheap American cotton imports eventually made linen less competitive. The last working flax mill in England closed just over ten years ago. Most of the mills turned to hemp in the nineteenth century but Metcalfe's at Glasshouse delayed the change and so became uneconomical. Pateley Bridge had two breweries and several inns, so many that a temperance house was set up in the town to counteract their attraction by serving cocoa.

Original shop displays and reinstated offices always fascinate museum visitors. These are wonderful at Pateley Bridge. The shelves in the general store are lined with toffee tins, bags of flour, chocolate boxes, potions and old cigarette packets and recall the art of the biscuit tin. This shop is filled with items which came with a complete shop, hence the quantities rather than single packets.

Together with a cobbler, in the same family for three generations, there is a chemist, a solicitor and the Mudd family which who made butter. There is an image of the butter sculpture flowers behind glass and without the benefit of freezers that won Miss Mudd prizes at the national dairy exhibition. This trade blossomed with the railways, making it easier to send milk out of the dales. The tradition of butter and cheese making continues at Kirkby Malzeard.

The town is not sophisticated, a market town since 1324 with a steep main street with hotels and shops. There are two excellent butchers, a grocer and hotel that serves the sort of meal JB Priestley would have indulged in: roast beef, Yorkshire pudding, vegetables, fruit pie and cream. The townscape is pleasant: there are carved porches, the odd Venetian window, with courts and alleyways to explore. The ruins of a fourteenth-century church stand at the top of the town which has a reputation for bedecking itself with flowers in hanging baskets to greet the summer and the visitors it brings.

39

Wensleydale

North Yorkshire

Wensleydale takes its name from a small village, but the River Ure is the principal river into which many tributaries feed and which this journey encounters with more water at Aysgarth Falls. The scenery takes in spectacular long-distance vistas of the fells to the north and south, castles and a cluster of busy centres. The valley fed by the Ure between Norton Conyers and Masham, my first stop is rich and park-like; after Jervaulx and Middleham the fells add their darker hues to the overall picture and then the stone walls take over.

I like Masham, the first town travelling in a westerly direction, it seems to be content. Masham is unassuming and epitomises the culture of a Yorkshire market town where farmers meet, exchange, sell and socialise. The church has Saxon foundations and its spire rises above a gentle landscape and dominates a very large market place. This, I was soon to realise, was no ordinary market place, but had been the premier selling arena for sheep farmers. It is surrounded by inns with a central cross and a variety of Wensleydale vernacular buildings. The King's Head hotel has a slate roof, some houses have tall chimneys and the virginia creeper covering the post office, when compared with early post-cards, has not changed since the 1920s.

Although the sheep auctions are no longer held here, in the 1950s the selling prices fixed the expectation for the year ahead as it was the first auction of the season. Now every autumn a large special breeds fair fills the whole square. I whiled away an afternoon here. Each lane and alley was filled with activities and with by-products; I came across a lean-to with outside tables weighed down with sheep skins in every shade of cream and brown. The amazing rare breeds are contained in long lines of pens, in some cases stretched taut by the girth of one single beast: Hebridean, Manx, the deep fudge-coloured Lochtan, with its four horns, Lincoln long wools and of course the black-face dales bred. The rain was not a deterrent; families and farmers were out for a weekend of tradition and festivity. I remarked to one that the sight of fine sheep makes one remember the astute monks and their granges, especially Fountains Abbey just nearby; 'what grazing country' I said; and he replied: 'if we didn't have the rain we wouldn't have the pasture!' Of course. At Masham I saw my first sighting of an authentic helping of Yorkshire pudding, almost fitting Priestley's description of a 'pudding that looks like a puff ball rather than a slice of a damp flannel'.

I visited one of the large auctions at Hawes the next day, having been advised by other guests at the farm where I stayed who were Leicesteshire farmers up to buy gimmers (young breeding ewes) to do so. At the Mart, the sounds of selling and the purpose of the town's origin thrives, and yet it is an ever increasing precarious living which has to come right. Coincidentally the farmhouse where we met had been built by a retired sailor in the nineteenth century on the highest piece of land so that he could see the masts at Whitby.

After Masham the landscape changes and once you pass the ruins of Jervaulx, open but owned privately, the road opens up towards Leyburn and Hawes beyond in the west. I had to stop at East Witton, a pretty neat village which was rebuilt twice, and has the essential qualities of the Picturesque with two almost continuous rows of stone houses, some terraced, some attached, built around an ellipsoidal green. This is a village to which the farmers retire. The monks of Jervaulx Abbey were granted a charter in 1306 to hold their market here although the original village was not on this site, it had been moved when they built anew on the axis of the abbey. The church, however was built much later in 1809 in stone by the Earl of Aylesbury, who also rebuilt the village.

Next, I lingered at Middleham Castle, half hidden in a mist, with no sunshine in it on that day. I was alone except for the ghosts. I tried to imagine the sounds and atmosphere of the fourteenth and fifteenth centuries, with Richard III's memory, and the odd contrast on that occasion of the history reinterpreted in a display of modern sculpture among the ruins and the rain. The Nevilles also had a reputation for giving feasts in Yorkshire, some lasting several days. As many as 2000 guests were invited where the accepted good manners would include: 'Byt not thy brede and lay it down', or rather break do not bite the bread, and 'ne suppe not with grete soundynge', eat quietly. Both have a familiar ring. Courses could well have numbered three, yet within each course there would be at least another seven dishes. Boars head might be served first with a kind of Yorkshire pudding to follow.

Middleham was much brighter on the following morning as the strings of thoroughbreds rode out against the high fells on the horizon. A cross still stands at Middleham which hosted one of the largest moors fairs held in the North. It was on the A684 to Hawes from East Witton that I first became fascinated by the stone walls, and started to photograph their detail. The regional differences are worth considering. In this part of the Dales the keystones are prominent, set repeatedly at right angles in the walls to give them strength. W G Hoskins, in his seminal work The Making of the English Landscape, tells us that these walls had a medieval origin. They were built as solutions to clear up the disputes between the tenants of the different abbey foundations, and that the tenants were in dispute until 1279 when the boundary walls were used.

Everyone stops at Aysgarth Falls, and so did I. This is a romantic setting as well as the site of the carriage museum; an old eighteenth-century cotton mill, built in 1787, extended in the nineteenth century, on the apex of the bend in the road opposite the falls. Among the sixty different carriages is a 250-year-old mail coach with extraordinary springing. Salmon were once caught in the Ure opposite, one weighing twenty pounds in the early 1800s, by Charles Fothergill who liked his food. The Falls halted the salmons' journey from the south, making it easy work for poachers to snatch fish from the roots of the trees.

I have three strong memories of Hawes apart from the sheep auction. One is the second-hand bookshop at Kit Calvert's where I found a copy of Oswald Harland's book on North Yorkshire. I tasted a cheese and butter tart at Elijah Allen, a grocer, established in 1868, and my visited Outhwaites the rope makers. Elijah Allen's is food heritage; although the interior has been streamlined, the windows are still original and are filled with rows of glass shelves. Thirty years ago every town had a proper grocery store like this, they often had a first floor restaurant or wood-panelled tea room. Allens sells locally made jams and curds and their curd tarts have won a regional competition. Wensleydale cheese is made in Hawes at the creamery, saved from closure a few years ago, after a public outcry; Ribblesdale comes from Ashes Farm and Swaledale from Richmond and homemade breads are also on sale. Allens bake the hams here, and sell local sausages and vegetables well set out; their paper bag, with the word purveyor emboldened, with a map of the area and cheeses, was my souvenir. Yorkshire cheese is in a league of it own; needing no more than good bread or a piece of Yorkshire apple pie, preferably of the ancestral variety.

In my search for other travel writers' memories of food I found that in 1805 Charles Fothergill described his dinner at the Wensleydale fair, where people generally kept open house, covering the table with good viands. He also recorded the dinner he ate near Middleham at the Judges' table where he had an excellent 'Sunday Dinner of venison, other game and dainties'. Hawes also appears to have had a tradition of good food and hospitality, especially good beef. The custom was to eat beef on special occasions, yet recipes for mutton hams and pies are rife in the northern books. My aromatic memory is of Outhwaithes whose rope works is in the centre of the town. Touring this factory took me back to my childhood, visiting and working as a student in my father's knitting factory, where it was wool, not hemp that was wound on to bobbins. Flax was the original crop in this region, now imported hemp was being wound on to long plastic cones, which used to be made in wood. As many as three hanks were being wound on to six cones to get the necessary thickness, for ships, industry and anywhere for which the strength of rope is needed.

Hawes is a workaday town, grey with its millstone grit and twisting, turning and narrow cobbled lanes down which I found the small sign for Kit Calvert's, the bookshop, engendering the anticipation of a find. I did not see the kind of scholarly gentlemen that Oswald Harland saw in 1946: 'tweed middle age and the young folk in flannels and corduroys', perhaps October was too late for this species. But I did see plenty of the nineties equivalent clothing – leggings. On the return to the end of the Dale I went to Leyburn which has two squares, one cobbled, graceful houses, and a small 1920s cinema with its original graphics, but have yet to see the town on market day.

As one approaches the eastern end of the dale the land becomes arable again. At Walburn Farm with its oriel windows and hood moulds, an unusual fortified farmhouse of the four-teenth century, the owner, Diana Greenwood, explained why there is such a pride in the roadside verges; I discovered that there is a healthy competition between Northumberland and Yorkshire. And then, if there is time, pause as I did at Constable Burton Hall, but a short distance beyond Leyburn and designed by John Carr.

This is a visit for garden lovers. There is no one on the gate, just an honesty box and a list of the plants and separate garden walks which they call 'stops'. An acer walk is for spring and autumn, the middle terrace has exceptionally large lilies in the summer, and a clematis Montana while 'Granny's garden' is a pot pourri with sweet peas. The semi-wild flower meadow was replete with willowherb while bridges spanned the small brooks. Constable Hall has a grand border with, among many other blooms, sedums, potentilla and roses. There is composure and structure in the rock garden and at the bottom a ravine and a fern garden. Everywhere one encounters discreetly placed seats, old walls, a lake and a garden for children all make this one of those gardens that needs several visits.

By way of a coda, Burneston, a small village, is an architec-tural reward on the way back to the A1 noted for its enchanting almshouses and church. These are quite grandiose almshouses for their position and were the gift of a Mr Robinson, the incumbent in 1680, who provided the money for this enchanting row of brick houses near the church. One of the present almoners took me in and showed me the parlour and stairs and told me that those who were lucky enough to meet the requirements had to live a sober life and help the church.

40

Wharfedale

North Yorkshire

There may not be as many villages in the Yorkshire dales as there are in the Cotswolds but the beauty of East Witton, Kettlewell and Coxwold equal any southern competitor. Here the farmsteads are spread out and the grazing is large-scale. Although other counties have stone walls, this one has a complete distinction. A tingle of excitement runs down my spine when I see the first flush of those wonderful vernacular stone barns filled with sweet-smelling hay. Why so many? Who built them? Whoever and whenever, they were needed to feed the stock in winter, Today these buildings verify the landscape which the miles of running stone walls frame.

There is a cluster of appealing churches in Wharfedale and Langstrothdale which warrant making a journey: each stop is an episode in itself. The diocese of Bradford has compiled a small useful leaflet, subtitled 'Stones that speak', and they do. I particularly wanted to see Hubberholme, on the northern extreme of this journey; the village seemingly abuts the edge of the world and is, and was, loved by many including J B Priestley whose ashes are scattered nearby. This excursion could be combined with Parcevall Hall gardens, Skipton or the Bolton Abbey Estate.

St Michael and All Angels at Hubberholme is a remote church with a good porch at the far reaches of Wharfedale, slotted in at the foot of the fells next to a farm beside the bridge. The tower is squat and the rare rood loft, is one of only two in Yorkshire of the mid-1550s to survive; it was once a forest chapel built by William de Percy and given to Coverham in 1241. There still stands the pub opposite where Priestley and his Bradfordian friends had lunch in October 1933 of soup, Yorkshire pudding, roast chicken, sausages, vegetables, fruit pudding, cheese and biscuits with coffee, and all for 2/6d each.

Priestley's journey in the autumn of 1933 in his beloved Yorkshire gave him veiws of the dales which were and still are past belief. Trees 'dripped gold'. I had been directed here one spring after Grassington by an engaging dales farmer, confessed retired, as I stopped to look at the roadside daffodils. He was out in the company of his dog checking his sheep which can suffer from a calcium deficiency that has to be remedied immediately. He urged me to go to Hubberholme, further up the dale. The road takes a more rugged turn after Conistone and Grassington, more austere, with fewer trees than Bolton. We chatted: 'You look like a professional woman', he said. When I described my mission he was delighted, eager to point me elsewhere in the county, and to this dale for which he exuded pride. Above all he insisted I see Swaledale, but not on that tour. I came back later in high summer for the wild-flowered dale.

The farmer's church at Conistone and his barns were to be noted. What I was planning met his approval. It was 'reet'. Our gossip covered everything from mules – sheep which are one year old, to literature and the price that rams fetch at Hawes. We could have gone on all evening, but his patient dog was eager and his last words still ring: 'Come back in June and I will show you the lady's slipper orchid.'

In the early nineteenth century Whitaker's illustration of the extraordinary hanging Kilnsey Crag, further south, was devoid of even a farmhouse; the low lying land was part of the abbey granges where sheep were sheared. This bizarre limestone promontory runs for a quarter of a mile along the valley, towering 165 feet high, more Wyoming than Yorkshire. On the way to Parcevall Hall I saw Linton's church, also dedicated to St Michael. For Whitaker, it was a 'solitary situation', and one must drive down, or better walk through the village to find the church and its two neighbouring houses, two parsonages nearly adjoining one another. There were two incumbents, bringing two sets of tithes who took it in turns to preach at the pulpit. Linton is an elegant little church situated by the Wharfe, which runs quieter here than Bolton, a Brontë novel setting if ever I saw one.

St Michael's huddles with the landscape, the Wharfe burbles beyond with a four-storey mill nearby. There is good wrought-iron work in the small, graceful bell tower, and the porch is Norman, it is a perfect piece of vernacular architecture. Because of St Michael's isolation beyond the village it was probably a pagan shrine. But Linton was wealthy; the spinning of hemp or flax gave the name with the spinners working in their own houses. Each house in the mid-1700s also had its own milk cow, fatted up a pig and kept sheep, being quite self-sufficient. Oats were dried or 'parched' in a common kiln, the place being the forerunner of the coffee house where gossip was exchanged and politics were debated over bread and oatmeal cakes. Each farmer brewed his own beer from barley and malt; meat was rarely eaten except on feast days, cheese was made on the farm and Whitaker also describes an early pasteurisation process.

Linton's wide, low profile fits the setting perfectly: Priestley's dripping gold beech trees making a resplendent frame for the building. The interior is a meld of Norman chancel arch and English Perpendicular aisle windows. The village also boasts some rather grand architecture including the resplendent Kirk Yett (is this a Viking word?) cottage. The fells beyond the Wharfe rise gently, at first higher on the horizon, with walkers ascending upwards like so many dots speckling the horizon.

Further along the river, St Wilfred's at Burnsall has an exceptional double hanging lych gate operated by a pulley. This may be one of the oldest churches founded by the Romille family. As the inscription says, it was 'butified' in 1612 by Sir William Craven, who also donated the grammar school next door. This church has a good ceiling, some Jacobean carving on the pulpit, encaustic tiles and a choir stall given by Sir Christopher Fountain, presumably from Fountain Hall at Linton. Those seeking grandeur will not find it these churches, the grandeur comes from the setting, the history, the endowments and the real purpose of place.

41

Whitby

North Yorkshire

Christianity, explorers, enlightenment and literature course through the veins of the town of Whitby. The sea is central to Whitby, with its intriguing mix of lanes (yards), cliffside terraces and harbourside weather boarded buildings. And above, the crenellated, ruined abbey dominates, high on the cliffs, a point of reference, as I approached across the ling-covered North Yorkshire moors.

Whitby harbour is a natural divide in the cliffs at the mouth of the River Esk, opening into the North Sea and giving the town its authority in the world of shipping and discovery. Where once the coble, a flat-bottomed boat, went out under brown sail, now diesel powers what is left of the fishing fleet. Today there are coasters but few trawlers working this stretch of the North Sea, and no one trades in whale, spices and wine, or trades out wool, leather and linen.

Whitby was never a parading place like Scarborough; it is more down to earth, more a coast town than a spa, and without pretence. It is a shipping, fishing and voyaging-out-from sort of place, whose yards and alleys, one felt, might still hold some undiscovered secrets.

The town's heyday was the eighteenth century but until the mid-nineteenth century it harboured as much as 1300 tons of shipping. In 1863 its lead in the shipping league fell to 500 tons with competition from industrial Middlesborough. But Whitby is really renowned for its port and for Captain Cook. He was a determined explorer and navigator, of whom his commander wrote 'neither danger nor fatigue could stop him'. For nine years Cook lived here, making his first voyage in the Endeavour, a refitted coal barque. The Whitby cats, or ships, that were built here, included the Resolution and the Endeavour.

James Cook was born in Marton, Cleveland, and worked in a grocery store in Staithes. He learnt his seagoing skills in the North Sea, studied mathematics by night and set standards of care for his crew, preventing scurvy by stocking the ship with cress, sauerkraut and a kind of extract of orange. Indeed, a man ahead of his times.

The four-storeyed house in Grape Lane, now the Captain Cook Memorial Museum, is predominantly seventeenth-century, with Elizabethan origins and a pantile roof. It is best seen from the harbour side; the town side is brick, painted deep red, the windows are picked out and there is a delightful spider's web fan-light above the front door. This house is one of the most exquisite small museums I have ever seen. It was the home of the sea master John Walker, a Quaker, and here Cook learnt his skill as an apprentice. The ground floor rooms are calm, small and pan-elled, the green room or dining room has wide pine planks and elegant plaster swags, and the little morning room, overlooking the harbour, is painted in a pale, forget-me-knot-blue, subtly con-trasting with the oak and cane high-backed chairs of the late sev-enteenth century. While this room provides an intimate view on to the street at ground floor level, there is a private view of the dining room from the street. Fortunately, the views are not over compromised by a new container building piercing the skyline beyond the harbour.

Equally well proportioned rooms on the first and second floors are cleverly lit and show models of the famous ships, doc-uments and prints. Botanical drawings by Parkinson for Sir Joseph Banks, the eminent botanist who sailed with Cook on his first voyage, underline the importance of the voyages that sought, recorded, and brought back evidence of this natural new world to England. Parkinson alone completed more than 200 botanical drawings that were later made into engravings, while other artists worked up his incomplete drawings under the direction of Banks. This type of expedition, a real voyage of discovery, was the model for the management of Charles Darwin's voyages in the following century. The artefacts are beautifully displayed, for example a garment called a chalket cloak, woven by North American Indians, was obtained by Cook. The cloak had been woven in bark fibre, but the method of weaving is almost mod-ern, or is it that this fundamental method is the same anywhere in the world? My lasting memory is of the attic where Cook and seventeen other apprentices slept between voyages. This is ship-timbered and left uncluttered save for a changing yearly exhibition set around the walls and focusing on different aspects of the discoverer's life. It is a tremendous space: white-washed, brick chimney breasts and wide floor timbers. Other houses might take note; not all rooms have to be filled to tell a historic story.

Queen Victoria's fashion for wearing Whitby jet during her mourning for Prince Albert helped to make the town fashionable and successful. Thus Whitby boomed in the 1860s, supplying jewellery to other European courts. Take any of the lanes off the harbour and you will find shops full of antique pieces which are very often intricately carved: brooches, necklaces, earrings. The old pieces now fetch very high prices because the trade declined when the fashion for mourning wear changed; but some of the modern workshops have started to produce again. Jet stone links fashion back to the Jurassic period, 200 million years ago, when decaying trees formed grey-blue mud and quartz stone which was covered again, and drifted to this area. The Whitby Museum also shows the geology and not only jet, but alum and the story of potash, mined at Boulby Cliffs, which was exported. And here also is most of a wing devoted to Captain Cook.

Vernacular customs often reach a higher status; Whitby is famous for its ganseys which are tough jumpers, hand-knitted in the round without seams to keep out the weather. Each fishing village on the North Sea had its own pattern. 'Whitby man' could be identified by the design of flags, ropes and steps: navy for every day, cream for Sunday best. You can now buy ganseys to wear on land or kits for knitting them up at home from Bobbins, a knitters' paradise selling only natural fibres, cotton and wool and all needs, in an old Wesleyan Chapel, replete with organ, in Church Street.

And so the continuing study of early Christianity in the North: at Whitby Caedmon, who was possibly the first composer of sacred songs, worked and sang for the Benedictine monks at the abbey in 657, later becoming a monk himself. His life was recorded by the chronicler Bede, and the Bodleian library in Oxford has a ninth-century copy of his poems.

Whitby also connects us with time and the calendar as we know it today, for it was here that the Synod of Whitby met in 664 and decided upon the day for celebrating Easter and the precise form of worship that would take place, and still does in the Church of England.

For the last 200 hundred years Whitby has been a catalyst for literary expression: Bram Stoker's Dracula, Storm Jameson, and Leo Walmsley's novels, Walter Scott's Marmion, and Wilkie Collins' No Name, one of the most beautifully crafted novels of Victorian social realism. In Whitby contrasts and traditions continue; on the road up to the abbey a picturesque assortment of buildings has grown up without lip service to any new southern style sheds. This is semi-detached housing for pigeons and the impedimenta of digging, a perfect alliance of vegetables and birds, high on the cliffs.

At the seaside the day should include fish. You can buy kippers at Fortunes in Henrietta Street at the foot of the 199 steps leading up to the abbey, where they smoke the herrings. Little has changed here either as they still smoke the 'silver darlings', now imported from Iceland, in a mixture of pine, beech and oak chippings. It was too soon after breakfast for some real Yorkshire fish and chips, the variety that should be lying on grids, brown and hot, dripping with fat, chips swimming in vats of boiling oil.

Fish and salt were the principal supplies transported on packhorse roads to the monks of Glaisdale Priory, who also walked to Whitby along the stone slab pavements just wide enough for one man to walk or ride a pony. And there are the remains of Wade's Causeway, a Roman road linking with Glaisdale on the Esk, which is another conjunction of industry and religion and famed for the best salmon fishing in England. Today it might be less stressful to take the North Yorkshire steam railway which runs from Pickering to nearby Grosmont, change to the Eskdale line and then to Whitby. There is no sound of industry today, it is still as Oswald Harland described his own North Yorkshire Moors in 1945, 'an excellent jumping off point for an excursion into the wilderness'.

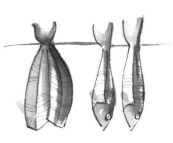

42

Yorkshire Country Wines, Glasshouses

North Yorkshire

As you drive out of Pateley Bridge towards Harrogate after a really engrossing museum tour, the first right turn for Glasshouse Mill is the prelude to a surprise. The nineteenth-century mill sits besides a bridge crossing the river Nidd. Once, more than 400 people were employed in making flax. Mrs Burgess has made a special study of the Metcalfe family, who owned the mill, and its position in the industrial scheme of things of this dale. At Glasshouse Mill school, where she taught, children once took lessons for only half the day – the other half was spent at the mill.

Yorkshire Country Wines make their wine here from fruits, flowers and vegetables. with such old-fashioned mixtures as parsnip and raisin, dandelion, gooseberry, cherry, blackberry and, of course the ever-popular, elderflower and elderberry. Richard Brown buys as much as locally as possible, and picks his own elderflowers to make cordial just for the tea room, in the vale of York in the early summer, moving nearer to his own valley or the hills beyond as the seasons progress. The family has been making the wines for several years and has opened one of the best tea rooms.

The Browns were clever with the location and in finding a building which lent itself so well to production and to the serious business of spoiling its visitors. The approach involves almost squeezing past the side of the mill with the river tumbling along on your right through a halcyon hideaway terrace, with old country garden furniture and stone slab tables, leading either to the winery or to the elegant tea room through French windows.

The winery is open to visitors. The original mill was supplemented by a huge turbine, on view through a glass floor panel which powered the mill in its heyday; this area is now the tasting area. The tea room is painted golden, the furnishings are simple, the eye is encouraged to travel outside and engage with an idyllic vista of the river and fields with cows grazing on the opposite bank. Extra light has been gained through top lighting, elegant light fittings and making the most of the windows. The little snug-like rooms are furnished with a mixture of country antiques and candlelit when necessary; leading off the conservatory they create a different mood. In the undercroft, running parallel to the tea room, are displays of country antiques and some charming drawings of the former mill. Elegant and intimate. This is unpretentious and there are no posies, but there is a style and polish not usually seen in the equivalent farm shop tea rooms. It was difficult to tear oneself away. I wanted to home up here for the afternoon after a walk in the dales.

There are three distinct eating areas: a small nook no larger than the table itself, half-curtained as for a private sitting for four, looking directly towards the high river bank, then a small candlelit room of country furniture seating about twelve and the conservatory. Such is their fame that some folk walk for miles to feast here. I wish that I did not have to travel 200 miles for another helping of this great food. The cakes? I am saving these, but they are worth waiting, walking and even riding for.

Their menu is thoughtful and distinctive; the dishes are carefully chosen to show off the region. There are the dales' cheese – Coverdale and Wensleydale from Newton le Willows the best I have ever savoured – served with three different chutneys from Darley: plum and orange and apple and ginger were two that I sampled. Ham and bacon is bought from Weatherheads in Pateley Bridge, who also cure. One of the inventive touches is the herb and cheese bread, made without yeast and served with every dish, be it soup, ham, cheese or light hot gratin. These light dishes such as broccoli, apple and Coverdale soup flag up the season. Leeks in their season with hazelnuts were crunchy and well furnished with a generous nut base. Service is informal, with pleasant young staff, yet has a nicety and each dish is served and presented on white china.

And so to the cakes, anticipate and imagine this. First blackcurrant pie or sticky gingerbread, and an apple tart, where the bramley apples have an exceptional character, having been lovingly turned in butter to keep their texture and appleness, one of the best confections I have met in the autumn, so good that I ordered a whole cake in advance for my next visit. And next a chocolate cake that was more a mousse captured between a delicate layer of coffee and pastry, light in texture and colour, deep in taste but not cloying. And for a Yorkshire pièce de résistance, a fruit cake soaked in rum, not drowned, served of course with a piece of the famous Wensleydale. There are three kinds of scones, cheese, cherry and bran and fruit, and their own elder-flower cordial was crisp, tart and refreshing. But maintaining this kind of quality requires the owners' presence, and I do hope that Mrs Brown's mother, whom I met, is training one or two with the required Yorkshire light baking hand to carry on with this trea-sure house of baking.

43

Fairfax House

York

Fairfax House is Georgian elegance done to a turn. This is a house whose survival and remarkable presentation is due to an unusual turn of events. Who on earth could envisage that a house could survive in spite of it being used as a cinema, a dancing school and a Friendly Society office and meeting room? But in fact all these uses enabled it to withstand a potential assault from a nearby development.

The refurbishment of the house in 1760 mirrored the digni-fied classical elegance. Robert Adam also worked in Yorkshire, but Fairfax is the work of a Yorkshire man, John Carr, whose oeuvre shines in York and elsewhere in the East Riding. A tea room would be superfluous here; nonetheless there are food connections enough to tickle all tastebuds and senses.

The house, as we shall see, was built solely for entertaining and hospitality, an enduring theme of the decoration and collection and through marvellous exhibitions held annually such as Keeping of Christmas, when the eighteenth century is perfectly recreated with a replica of York's first Christmas tree, table size, and possibly the only time visitors are given mulled wine and mince pies. Another exhibition takes place in between the festive seasons. I recently saw Pleasures of the Table, where setpiece displays were based around archival evidence and images of parties. One food picture, a replica in sugar paste of a parterre garden in fruit, was set out geometrically, with pears, Ribston pippins, peaches, oranges and flowers; another as for dessert with chocolate puffs and sugar paste figures from Greek mythology. One of the bedrooms showed the whole equipage for tea-taking and the drawing room displayed the fashion for card-playing with a table set out for drinking punch and playing. These exhibitions unite the Georgian period with contemporary decorative arts, food and style of entertaining.

Fairfax House was saved by the York Civic Trust with consummate skill and great dedication. The restoration took place under the guidance of another York architect, Francis Johnson, whose twentieth-century work is as significant to York's architectural fabric as Carr's is to its eighteenth-century Georgian buildings. The restoration is enhanced by a permanent collection of exceptional quality given by the trustees of Noel Terry, the chocolate manufacturer, as he wished it to remain in the city.

Before you enter the rich, contrasting entrance, with deep red brick and cream stone quoins around the windows, ponder the fact that this house once stood alone in a prime location between the two rivers and looking over gardens with a view down to the Ouse, although Castlegate House, also Carr's, was built in about 1770. Fairfax was built in about 1740 and then bought by Lord Fairfax for his daughter as a vehicle for entertaining and gaining her entry into society with the intention of finding a suitable husband. Anne Fairfax had already experienced two thwarted romances, including a last-minute cancellation of her wedding to William Constable of Burton Constable, another fine house in this county

Fairfax's entrance hall is designed to encourage and excite the visual senses through a series of arches, creating an ingenious passage through progressively ornate reception rooms. Mouldings and architraves are designed to intensify the light and prepare you for your arrival. But visitors should remember that they enter through what was later the cinema, not the original door. The plasterwork ceilings here and on the ceiling of the grand staircase and in what was the ballroom are regal, allegorical and symbolic, with motifs becoming richer as you travel through the house. Viscount Fairfax's royalist allegiance and Roman Catholic faith can be decoded in the decoration of the plasterwork. For both visitor and student of the Georgian style there is no better house for experiencing the age of elegance and equilibrium.

The possibilities of metaphor in design have been embraced by Carr to fulfil Fairfax's intentions; the plasterwork is iconographic and lavish with examples of Doric frieze or guillotting normally applied to the exterior of a house. Here, in the dining room,they become synonymous with outward elegance, so that, for example, one design symbolises fruitful harvests with carvings of Bacchus above the diner's head. And research has confirmed

that vast quantities of sack, port, Madeira, Lisbon and Frontignac, another form of port, were consumed at Fairfax dinner parties where none other than Laurence Sterne also dined, not as a writer or preacher but representing his patron, Lord Fauconberg.

The pièce de résistance in terms of carving and architectural drama is the staircase, which ascends importantly past a curved-headed Venetian or Serlio window to a landing with ornate doors and a ceiling of formidable stucco work. Together with Cortese, the master craftsman of stucco, Carr has achieved here in scale what is normally only seen in a large country house. For me the most entertaining ceiling was the drawing room where a perspective, not in painterly terms, has been accomplished using a coffered design with a coved border radiating to the centre. At first glance, it is disconcerting, but nevertheless charming and a good conversation piece.

Although the kitchen is not original, and may have been destroyed during the cinema conversion of the 1920s, it is a room in which I could happily cook, using the small table with its over-hanging top which seemingly converts to a bench in the unlikely event that there is time to sit, with a pot board underneath. As elsewhere, the furniture is contemporary and includes an eighteenth-century food or dole cupboard. Anne's bedroom on the first floor has an exquisite four-poster bed almost overburdened, yet invitingly generous with its flax-coloured cotton and linen covers and sheets. Also on this floor, in the later addition which became the cinema next door, yet connected to the main house, one finds a collection of silver, glass and decorative arts which with the Terry Collection of eighteenth-century furniture and other bequests complete the tour. Go and be prepared to drool.

44

Treasurer's House

York

There are many buildings with religious associations and foundations quite close to the minster and Minster Yard. Treasurer's House is one of these. The visible structure dates from the sixteenth century, but its position hints of a much earlier foundation. There are several additions and their sequence takes time to grasp. The National Trust, to whom the house was given in the 1930s is restoring the twentieth-century mantle with which Frank Green the industrialist imbued this elegant and complex house.

It was initially built for a canon treasurer, the keeper of all the cathedral accounts. It was saved by the fortune of Frank Green who was assisted by his architect Temple Moore. At Treasurer's House you get an architectural bonus by looking through the windows to the almost secret internal courtyard of Gray's Court next door also restored by Moore. This view of a curious cobbled yard with pollarded plane trees and a rich two-storey panelled porch with an oriel window, whose glass was designed by Knowles, (see page 170), reminds one of a sixteenth-century French place or square. And there is another piece of the vast Yorkshire jigsaw, this one is literary. Laurence Sterne's uncle Dr Jacques Sterne, who helped him to the living at Coxwold, lived at Grays Court in the 1740s. Perhaps Sterne stayed here when he dined at Fairfax House (see page 161).

Frank Green made his money from manufacturing boilers in Wakefield and restored the house in an eclectic manner, doubtless with his own ideas for decoration. The entrance hall is painted in a marvellous soft emerald green and the wall decoration verges towards trompe l'oeil, where contrasting vertical sections of the painted wall vie with the hatched black and white skirting boards.

As royalty was entertained in the early part of the twentieth century the servants had their place. Ground rules were laid down and posted in the kitchen where Green's portrait surveys the scene. We are informed that Princess Victoria's lady's maid ate in the servants hall and propriety reigns in the laundry lists where pantry cloths, eiderdown covers and staff face towels are all listed separately from the family. There is some unusual glass in the windows in this room with a rather odd, round etched pattern while Delft tiles are a handsome addition.

The accumulation of wealth and its custody underpin this building; successive owners no doubt brought their own ideas and unquestionably York was fashionable – Grand Tour ideas would have surfaced as much here as in London. Most of the doorways are ornate in French rococo style in particular the drawing room where the exquisite entrance has elaborate plasterwork. This room has a large fireplace with an ornate over-mantel. In the first-floor Tapestry Room hangs a beautiful piece of early sixteenth-century stumpwork with flowers, floors, buildings and clothes carefully worked, with a naive style. Altogether some exceptional design details have been left from the earlier building: the reverse curved balustrades are witty and so is the fluted newel post. The bay window with its Chippendale seat looks out on Gray's Court and a charming collection of pottery in vivid coloured pearlware with incised lines in green with a contrast tortoiseshell base and elegant silver top is shown.

Treasurer's House is a house from which you look out at York as well as inside it. From the important Venetian windows in the principal bedroom there is a grand circle view of the chapter house and minster and from the most intimate room of all, the card room on the ground floor, more Jacobean than the others there is a private theatre-box view of the chapter house. At one time a row of houses blocked the view that Green made so much of. Looking down inside the house a minstrels' gallery overlooks the great hall and a huge buffet in Elizabethan revival style.

I particularly admire the plethora of Venetian windows in the lower hall and above. There are tapestries and nooks to explore, but in order to read the different periods of the building and appreciate the whole facade you need to stand with your back to the chapter house. From here you can appreciate the H plan, the two wings with their fenestration and the centre block which contains the great hall with its early sixteenth-century entrance, the windows and shaped gables were added 100 years later.

There is a tea room below stairs in what was once the undercroft, with white-washed walls, beech furniture and a fair selection of cakes on the dressers. The room feels fresh and inviting. The contemporary prints and fresh flowers add to the atmosphere and there are hints and flavours of this county. Parkin can be found, and for Yorkshire cheese addicts there is no shortage: a selection is served with bread which you can taste with one of the excellent Yorkshire country wines. Sandwiches are filled with York ham and the rest of the menu is unfussy: fresh soup, say lentil and tomato in autumn, and a light dish made with smoked mackerel, or perhaps a hot lemon pudding. Through an impressive studded door there is a second eating room where the staff also wait upon visitors in an equally welcoming manner.

45

St Martin's le Grand and
St Michael's Spurriergate

York

After walking the length of Stonegate, through St Helen's Square, then past the arch and entrance to the Guildhall, bombed in 1942 and since restored, move on to Coney Street where there is a little gem. I urge you to see the cleverly restored south aisle of St Martin's le Grand, its unrestored ruins surrounded by railings and a large proud seventeenth-century clock hanging over Coney Street. This was an early post-Conquest church, principally built in the fifteenth century, having the good fortune to be reconstructed after the Second World War by George C Pace in 1968. I found it hard to believe that York suffered quite so much in the air raid of 1942, part of the Baedeker raids which were directed at many other historic cities such as Canterbury and Norwich.

The restoration took seven years to complete and indeed, the whole assembly of fittings, seventeenth-century altar table, special stained-glass window detail, with one of the finest, writes Pevsner, font covers in York, are housed in the remains of a very small church. Pace designed the railings which lead you through a wrought-iron gate but also the interior which incorporates his own fittings such as the organ case which is unique as it hangs from the arches to give a view of the west window. The modern stained glass by Henry Stammers and the sculpture by Frank Roper combine well with the soft limed oak pews. Two services are held here each week without, I imagine, any pomp, rather, I suspect, a friendly intimate atmosphere, if my experience in the small refectory was significant.

The staircase leading upstairs has been cleverly resolved in oak with slender squint windows: the wooden screen at the top is also elegantly executed. The small refectory, only open on Saturdays, is white-washed with views on to the back of the church. The welcome is authentic, the value unbeatable, and the service simple. Where else could you get a very good cup of coffee and a date cake for £1 in a city centre? Soup, they confessed is not homemade, for there is nowhere to cook. But there are plenty of cakes: ginger, coconut slice, scones, date and walnut cake with scones or ham rolls. From the wooden tables there is a just enough view over the roofs to put one in touch with York at another level. And the merry company of helpers of all ages work behind the counter maintaining a stream of news and exchanges with the visitors. In turn, friends or those in the know, both up here and in the church, make it just as lively as it should be.

I found St Michael's in Spurriergate located at the end of Coney Street, equally inviting although larger. This church has been converted into a centre following the traditions of hospitality in monastic guest houses. The cornerstone of Christian belief, pastoral care and outreach are combined with food and trading, and although St Michael's does not hold any formal services, the involvement of those who work here forms a connection between church and community. Once a month the café closes for quiet days and the staff hold a small prayer meeting each day in which anyone can take part.

A church stood here before William the Conqueror reached York. In spite of new walls and alterations over the last 170 years, many of the interior fittings have been highlighted in another of George Pace's restoration of the 1960s. The aisles are wide, and one can see elements of the twelfth century, the fifteenth and the early eighteenth centuries. The reredos is classical and quite beautiful, thought to be the work of the York woodcarvers John and William Etty, with an ornate central panel showing the Ten Commandments painted in gold also depicting St Michael slaying the dragon while the side panels have the Lord's Prayer and Creed, as churches were required to do, painted large for the congregation to see. Many people come to see the fifteenth-century Jesse window, but I have, in my mind, the seventeenth- century marble monuments, and the heavy studded west door behind the bell ropes. I cannot ever recall before eating lunch within sight of bell ropes. But St Michael's is after all the middle of a shopping thoroughfare and is therefore full of animated visitors on a Saturday. They are a happy crowd, and, the food is down to earth. Evidently they can never take Yorkshire pudding off the menu, as this would cause an outcry; apart for this almost national dish, there is homemade soup, three or four good salads and puddings, and mercifully they keep as much as possible going until later in the day. I had a very late lunch around four. Both the churches of St Martin's and St Michael's in their own fashion offer a sympathetic quality and another dimension to the shopping streets of York.

46

Stonegate, Coney Street and New Earswick

York

Y ork's architectural achievements surpass those of any other English city because its medieval heart was protected by a ring road. The remains chart both medieval and Georgian society, their power, wealth and fashion. Its sum gives great pleasure.

The ascendency of the fifteenth and early sixteenth-century merchants in York was a triumph. And the city acquired large parishes with as many as forty-five churches by 1300. York did, however, suffer from the Reformation when the population dipped, and it was bombed in the Second World War. Nevertheless, there are some of the very best examples of medieval shops in the whole country in Stonegate, where today's enjoyment is enhanced by the want of motorcars. This, like many other streets, is pedestrianised and is just as tempting to tread up and down in the evening, when the shop windows shine out.

The shops survive and timbering abounds because the merchant-owners chose to stay with their warehouses or shops in the city within the walls; Stonegate especially illustrates how businesses thrived as their premises grew in the narrow space. And they grew in the only possible direction by extending laterally at each of the upper levels or providing jetties until in one street, the Shambles, the opposite top stories almost touch each other.

Number 35 Stonegate, a whole street of shops, is a favourite, for its design and associations. It was altered by John Ward Knowles, a Victorian stained glass maker, designer and restorer whose monument is all around in York. He bought the shop after it had been the publishing house owned by Francis Hillyard in 1683, and where later Sterne's Tristram Shandy was published, although it actually began life as an abbot's house, part of the see of Durham in 1487. Knowles restored stained-glass for the minster, All Saints, Holy Trinity in Micklegate and St Lawrence's; most of the nineteenth and twentieth-century stained glass in York is by Knowles. Having bought number 35, in 1873 he redecorated and embellished the front, respecting the fifteenth-century design and the crown post. The yellow stained-glass panels with delicate sunflowers on the side of the ground-floor windows first caught my eye. Just below the level of the windows decorative panels give the date of 1874 after his refurbishment.

Mr Knowles' wife was not just an excellent needlewoman but also operated his business and design studio, selling church furnishing and furniture. In its own way it was a smaller-scale Morris and Co, with the shop as a showroom promoting good design. The shop front is an artwork in itself of decorated wood, glass, and tiles; climbing the steps reminds me of all those equally marvellous shops fronts which are now to a great extent lost.

Nikolaus Pevsner the most respected of architectural historians, describes number 37 next door of eighteenth and nineteenth centuries as the 'best shop front in York.' It is somewhat later than number 35 Stonegate and has fluted columns and large bow-fronted, chocolate-box windows. Yet there is more. Mulberry Hall is a mid-fifteenth century double-fronted building with jetties at each level. Every shop here would qualify as an exhibit in a museum, but this is the real thing. There are, however very few food shops. In the Shambles, originally called the Great Flesh Shambles in the fifteenth century, there were still twenty-five butchers' shops in 1872.

Timber-framed houses were far more flexible than the stone used in the eighteenth century. Castle Gate has the elegant town houses of Fairfax and Castle Gate House, beautiful evidence of York's rise as a place for society to frequent and be seen in. But all the courtyards – Coffee Yard and Barley Hall – and alleys still run straight from one to another between the former merchants houses, like overground street tunnels. The bliss of walking about York is that there is something for everyone in terms of architectural style. It is by no means all Gothic or Classical. There are revivals of both and examples of several different fashions.

First, in St Helen's Square, casting a glance at what was Terry's former large emporium, no longer selling chocolate but with the name still in stone, and then to Coney Street, good for building style spotters. Many of the modern shops conceal the original seventeenth and eighteenth-century buildings. But one also finds examples of early twentieth-century shop fronts. The heritage style of Boots was designed by Treleaven with its own 'black and white' in 1907, a corporate image used by them in other market towns and here making a very accomplished contribution to the Tudor revival of York. There is fine decoration and painted plasterwork, pargeting and a good clock. Burtons, on the other hand, of fifty shilling fame, still has its deco face, metal windows and familiar granite signature of 1931. Further down, in Coppergate, look at the first floor above Habitat which suggests that York tradespeople were aware again of the vogue. This elevation runs across three houses; on the right a late fin de siècle or rather a classic art nouveau motif of peacock panels on one side and two figures on the other.

York is remembered for the production of cocoa and chocolate but tons of butter were also exported from here at King's Staith which before the silting up of the Ouse was the main landing stage. Among the many thousands of remarkable buildings in the central core Bootham Hotel is worth seeing. It meets Bootham Bar at right angles and almost touches it at the top. But in York you are never far away from architectural reminders of the powerful Quaker families of Terry and Rowntree. They did not just make chocolate. Terry's, now Swiss-owned, was revered for the family's philanthropy. And the Rowntrees endowed public buildings – I saw the Joseph Rowntree Theatre on the road to New Earswick. Here they sponsored an enlightened and innovative scheme of social housing designed by Barry Parker and Raymond Unwin (of Letchworth Garden City fame), which is a complete garden village built for Rowntree workers. The design follows ideas for bringing sunlight into the houses, although they attracted opposition to their idea of omitting a parlour. The population was not quite ready for this in 1902.

But the houses seem as desirable today as they were when they were built with their own village hall and specially built shops. Each house had an open aspect and, following Ebenezer Howard's garden city plan, there are good gardens with small access avenues. They are family houses built in local materials with generous eaves and gardens. Even here York predates the rest of the country for its homes for its working heroes were built before the First World War to reduce the problems of poor housing in the nineteenth century.

47

York Minster, St William's College, the Merchant Adventurers Hall and York City Gallery

York

The twin iconic towers of St Peter's the York Minster draw everyone like a stone magnet to the close, a marvellous position to start a magnum walk of York. As for the minster, I prefer a late visit when the church is quieter. No one should hurry York – the streets, the Georgian houses, the guildhalls, the wealth, the minster or the City Art Gallery.

York Minster has been plundered and burnt in 1829, 1840 and not so long ago in 1984, and much restored. It is a church that had many new beginnings. First in AD71 it was a Roman site – the city of Eboracum – followed by the early Christian church founded in 627, refurbished by St Wilfrid of Hexham and Abbot of Ripon in 670, and described as 'a paragon of lofty beauty, supported by massive pillars' in the eighth century. The Saxon remains have not all been discovered, nor the remains of the first Norman church founded in 1090 (whose bishop was Thomas of Bayeux) where the walls were as wide as seven feet using both Roman and Saxon masonry.

Essentially York minster is Gothic, more English than Durham, with each progressive period of medieval style being embodied. The minster's magnificence is staggering. There is only one approach: go, enter and just stand, gaze and quietly try to absorb the volume, form, decoration and colour.

Much of the building as we see it dates from 1230 when Walter de Gray built anew with the intention of it being 'the greatest church built in the kingdom' and finished in 1472 in magnesium limestone from Tadcaster. The crossing tower, given by Bishop Skirlaw and constructed by William of Colchester who supervised Westminster Abbey, follows this as the second highest in England. The transepts are incomparable and there are two flying arches with extraordinary springing. The choirs are picked out in green and gold, with ornate carving, and the sumptuous west window completed in 1338 and paid for by Bishop Melton was described by Nikoluas Pevsner in his Buildings of England as having the finest medieval stained glass in England. I agree with Oswald Harland, a Yorkshire man, that 'seeing everything one remembers nothing', so I will pick out a handful of elements that particularly struck me.

First the towers themselves, which were completed at the end of the 200 years of building. These are Decorated and therefore different from other contemporary towers. And then the north transept where the height and delicacy of the Five Sisters windows, filling one wall, all the same size and all lancet-shaped, were fitted in 1260. The slenderness and height of 55 feet are awe inspiring, as is the marvellous stained glass in the great east window, a narrative art executed in 1408 and funded by Walter Skirlaw, Bishop of Durham (see page 118) who died in 1406 which shows him accompanied by York luminaries. This, and the rose window built to celebrate the union of the houses of York and Lancaster and the Five Sisters windows are essays in glass. The design for the carving of the choir screen is atributed to William of Colchester who succeeded the great master Yeveley who worked both on Westminster Hall and Canterbury. The screen of 1460 was, supposedly, made in London, modelled on a prototype and then painted in red and gold. The beautiful chapter house was once all wood. This was replaced by lathe and plaster by John Carr; the interior is unique being the only polygonal example without a central column.

Not only Carr but many other architects were invited to rework and restore this great minster over several centuries: Lord Burlington, Sir William Kent, Street, Sir Sydney Smirke (brother of Robert), Wyatt, Bernard Feilden in the 1960s and Sir Charles Brown between 1984 and 1988. Pevsner has thirty pages just on this exceptional example of the mastery of English medieval art and craft. For early music fans and drama devotees, the York festival in early summer offers medieval music and performances of medieval mystery plays, to be performed in the minster in 2000.

Minstergate is the best space in which to understand religious York, and the wonder of the minster. College Street runs off this yard with one of the last minster gateways or arches. I am in no way advocating passing by the other buildings in the yard for each one is worthy, but St William's College is deserving for its architecture and for the food. It lies east of the minster and was founded in 1455 as a home for the priests who sang in the chantry chapel, a York equivalent of, if not a few years older than, the Vicars' Close in Wells.

The Dean and Chapter are the trustees of St William's College which was built in 1461 as a home for chantry priests. It is viewed as the public refectory for the minster and was first set up in 1975 to cope with the increase in tourism and run by the same company which provide equally good food at the Railway Museum. The whole length of the timber facade is striking, a three-storeyed black and white building with an unusual coving under the jetty and oriel windows. These were rebuilt in 1902 by Temple Moore whose work can be seen at the Treasurer's House and Gray's Court close by and modelled on the last surviving original on the first floor. The ground floor is of ashlar stone with alternating eighteenth-century 'shop' bay windows. A central arch takes you into a large cobbled courtyard.

The house was once owned privately by the Earl of Carlisle, who acquired it after the dissolution of Chantries in 1547. It was bought back by the church in 1902. Once in the courtyard it is easier to make the contrast with the black and white timbered jetties of the first floor and the stone below, and this enclosed space deposits you into an intimate medieval space with the added privilege of being able to linger, admire and imagine medieval sounds and colours.

The refectory occupies three bays of the ground floor, with outside tables in the courtyard and College Street. The restaurant retains its original features. is divided into pleasing smaller spaces with fireplaces, and good furniture all candlelit in the evening with a view of the minster. And as this restaurant serves supper, one's history-visiting day can be stretched further. The food is consistently good, a Yorkshire flavour with fashionable style. There is celery soup on a winter's day and you might see a majestic York ham (the wood chippings from the building of the minster are allegedly what gave these hams their quality and fame). Roast meats are followed by excellent puddings. The foods enthusiastically served in season, using local producers, are leek and Wensleydale tart, brown bread ice cream, Ribblesdale and Lancashire cheese, banana and gingerbread cake, and a wonderful sounding Yorkshire grown rhubarb pudding, were offered one spring. The meringues are large, the salads are imaginative and vegetables are always of the season. York must be one of the few cathedrals where you can dine after your tour and they plan to change to table service making it a little more comfortable.

The guild halls make a link between secular and religious York. One hundred years after the Gothic minster was begun a group of highly placed citizens formed a fraternity and built the Merchant Adventurers Hall in Fossgate, a listed Grade I building, and an insight into the power of the guilds. By the mid-fifteenth century most of the members were wealthy merchants; and here they met, traded, and worshipped.

The Merchant Adventurers Hall is placed so that visitors can enjoy and walk around the whole building with its gardens and seats. The Hall is predominently brick and stone to the first floor made with some of the earliest bricks; the upper storeys are timbered with yellow lime-washed infill. The whole construction was set out, as many timber-framed houses were, marked then reassembled on to the brick base with each marked truss beam or post being matched together in situ. On the street entrance a fine stone arch leads to a gate house and the gabled building with elaborately carved barge boards. So often a historic building can be over interpreted, but this is not.

A handful of artefacts, silver, furniture, a magnificent spindlewood abbot's chair, an elegant eighteenth-century sign that tells where the high-water mark was in 1731, are enough. The star of the show is the timber framing, and the posts of the great hall and the undercroft. The hall hosted the guild meetings and the vast crown posts signify its importance. A classical style of podium with fluted columns painted pale contrasts to the oak floor. Portraits grace the walls. Then in the undercroft one is even more aware of the great timber posts. This housed thirteen poor people with a chapel at one end and one of surely the largest fireplaces outside a castle or baronial hall. An exceptional fireplace with four hearths and divided by a tiny passage was inserted in the sixteenth century. The decoration on the banners shows the different trades: cordwainers, glaziers, pewterers and grocers. Patronage and support are as strong today. The whole interior and exhibition are on display, except when the hall is being used for dinners.

I made some finds at the York City Art Gallery, whose decoration was never finished; a decorated frieze was planned which would have given it more of a chance against the ornate tricked-out doorway of its neighbour, the King's Manor. Almost opposite stands the eigthteenth-century Theatre Royal with an addition by the architect Patrick Gwynne in 1967; very much of its period, over-sailing and embracing the city in concrete and glass. But York City Art Gallery is a typical late Victorian museum, top-lit, and with a banquet of art from all periods.

Ceramics play an important part and the collection includes work by William de Morgan, his wonderful deep lustre blue and sunflower tiles. A room is devoted to the work of twentieth century potters including Bernard Leach, part of an exciting collection begun by Milner White in the 1920s when he was, unusually, collecting the work of many contemporary artists, and the work of Hamada the Japanese potter.

The City Gallery's strength lies in its eigthteenth-century work by Hogarth and Reynolds, a whole room is devoted to the works of William Etty who was born in York. The county and the artists who have been inspired by it are well represented. A picture of the Strid at Bolton Abbey by Etty in 1849 shows far more trees than today, while the work of artists who were equally moved by the ruins of Fountains Abbey can be seen. Among them is a Turner first exhibited 1798; he was less concerned with likeness than evoking the atmosphere. And in 1983 John Piper made a screen print which is an extraordinary bright green (he was colourblind). A still life from Ben Nicholson's prewar period joins in with the ceramics gallery and the work of Bernard Leach and Staite Murray. I continue to find works by other inter-war British artists in my travels, here was a Paul Nash: Winter Sea and a wonderful Tristram Hillier of hay-making in the war, stylised, with bright pink-painted carts.

I also found a bust of John Carr, the architect who was made an alderman and mayor. Nollekens' work shows his intensely intelligent looking face. York has a wide ranging collection enough to start a study of many periods. And that is about the truth of the city.

There is almost too much, you cannot afford to keep your face downwards (there are far too many cluttering A-boards) for fear of missing something. York is a jewel that requires much more than a single excursion. Happily it is also accessible, being the cradle of railway travel with a very fast service. Book a return journey for second helpings.

ABBOT HALL 1
Kendal, Cumbria LA9 5AL
TEL *01539 722464*
FAX *01539 722494*
OPEN *summer 10.30-5pm
winter 10.30-4pm
Admission charge
Tea room: free access,
seats 30
Disabled access at art
gallery, partial in museum,
WCs in coffee shop*
RAIL *Oxenholme*
ROAD *A591 M6
Disabled parking*

**APPLEBY-IN-
WESTMORLAND
TOURIST
INFORMATION
CENTRE** 2
TEL *017683 51177*

**CASTLE GATE
HOUSE GALLERY** 3
*Castle Gate House,
Cockermouth, CA13 9HA*
TEL *01900 822149*
OPEN *March-Dec except
Thurs and Sun
Disabled access: ring in
advance. Disabled parking
(See Wordsworth House
for transport details)*

**HIGH STANGER
FARM** 3
Cockermouth CA13 9TS
TEL *01900 823875*

AIRA FORCE 4
ROAD *A592*

DALEMAIN 4
Dacre CA11OHB
TEL *017684 86450*
OPEN *Easter-October
Sun-Thurs
Admission charge
Tea room seats 40
Disabled access to tea
room, partial to house*
RAIL *Penrith*
ROAD *A 592
Batricar for grounds*

BRIDGE HOUSE 5
*Rydal Road, Ambleside
Cumbria*
TEL/FAX *015394 32617*
OPEN *April-end Oct
Mon-Sun 10-5
Disabled access*
RAIL *Windermere*
BUS *555 and 599,
summer only*
ROAD *A591*

TOWNEND 5
*Troutbeck, Windermere
LA23 1LB*
TEL *015394 32628*
OPEN *Beg April-end Oct,
closed Mon and Sat
except Bank Holidays, 1-5
Admission charge*
NT *members free*
RAIL *Windermere*
ROAD *A591 and A592*

**KENDAL TOURIST
INFORMATION
CENTRE** 6
TEL *01539 725758*
FAX *01539 734457*

**THE PENNINE
POTTERY** 7
*Clargill Head House
Alston, Cumbria CA9 3NG*
TEL *01434 382157*
OPEN *Apr-Jan and Bank
Holidays 10–5.30*
RAIL *nearest Penrith*
ROAD *A686*

**ALSTON TOURIST
INFORMATION
CENTRE** 7
TEL *01434 381696*

**THE VILLAGE BAKERY
MELMERBY** 8
*Melmerby, Penrith
Cumbria CA10 1HE*
TEL *01768 881515*
FAX *01768 881848*
OPEN *Mon-Sat 8.30-5,
Sun 9.30-5. Seasonal
changes: Jan & Feb.
Phone for closing times
Tea room seats 45
Disabled access except
toilets*
RAIL *Langwathby (Carlisle
Settle Line) phone for lift,
Penrith main line*
ROAD *A686
Disabled parking*

WORDSWORTH HOUSE   **9**
*Main Street, Cockermouth
Cumbria CA13 9RX*
TEL *01900 824805*
OPEN *April-Oct weekdays
11-5. Phone for extra
weekend opening
Admission charge*
NT *members free
Tearoom seats 25*
OPEN *as house
Free access to tea room*
RAIL *Penrith to Workington*
BUS *Stagecoach
Cumberland X5*
ROAD *A66*

CLITHEROE TOURIST INFORMATION CENTRE   **10**
TEL *01200 425566*

GARSTANG TOURIST INFORMATION CENTRE   **10**
TEL *01996 602125*

GAWTHORPE HALL **11**
*Padiham, Nr Burnley
Lancs BB12 8UA*
TEL *01282 771004*
FAX *01282 770178*
OPEN *1 April-31 Oct 1-5
daily except Mon & Fri
Admission charge*
NT *members free
Tea room seats 40*

OPEN *12.30-5 when hall
open
Tea room access difficult
Disabled access limited*
RAIL *Burnley Central and
Burnley Barracks*
BUS *all pass Padiham*
ROAD *A 671
Disabled parking*

PENDLE HERITAGE CENTRE   **12**
*Park Hill, Barrowford
Nelson, Lancs BB9 6TQ*
TEL *01282 661702*
FAX *01282 611718*
OPEN *daily except
Christmas day 10-5
Admission charge to
house and garden
Free to gallery shop and
tea room
Tea room seats 75
Disabled access to lower
rooms garden, cruck barn
and tea room*
RAIL *Nelson and Burnley*
BUS *10 from Burnley
station*
ROAD *A 682 from M65
Disabled parking limited*

RIBCHESTER MUSEUM   **13**
*Riverside, Ribchester
Preston, Lancs PR3 3XS*
TEL *01254 878261*
OPEN *All year weekdays
9-5 weekends 12-5*

*Admission charge
Disabled access*
RAIL *Whalley or Preston*
ROAD *A59*

BACKFOLD COTTAGE   **14**
*The Square, Waddington
Lancs BB7 3JA*
TEL *01200 422367*
RAIL *Clitheroe*
BUS *From Clitheroe*

DURHAM CATHEDRAL   **15**
Durham DH1 3EQ
TEL *01913 864266*
OPEN *7.30am-5.30pm
Disabled access*
RAIL *Durham*
BUS *North Road bus station*
ROAD *A1
Disabled parking on
Palace Green*

THE ALMSHOUSES CAFE   **15**
*Palace Green
Durham DH1 3RL*
TEL *0191 386 1054*
OPEN *Easter to Oct 9-8
Winter 9-5
Seats 60
Disabled access*

LOW URPETH FARMHOUSE 16
Ouston, Chester-le-Street
Co. Durham DH2 1BD
TEL 01914 102901
FAX 01914 100081
OPEN all year except
Christmas
RAIL Newcastle or
Chester le Street
ROAD A1(M) then A167

HIPSBURN FARM HOUSE 17
Nr Alnmouth
Northumberland
NE66 3PY
TEL 01665 830206
RAIL Alnmouth
BUS Alnwick to Alnmouth
ROAD A1068

ALNWICK TOURIST INFORMATION CENTRE 17
TEL 01665 510665
FAX 01665 510447

CHESTERS ROMAN FORT 18
Chollerford
Northumberland
NE46 4EP
TEL O1434 681379
OPEN April-Sept every day
10-6, Oct 10-5
Nov-March 10-4
Admission charge
EH members free

Tea room seats 20
OPEN Summer
Tea room free access
Disabled access and
parking
RAIL Hexham 5.5 miles
BUS Phone 01670 533128
ROAD B6318 1.5 miles
west of Chollerford

CHILLINGHAM CASTLE 19
Chillingham
Northumberland
NE66 5NJ
TEL 01668 215359
FAX 01668 215463
OPEN May 1-Oct 1, 12-5.30
Closed Tues May, June,
Sept, Oct
Admission charge
Free to children
Tea room seats 50
OPEN 12.30-5.30
Disabled access difficult
RAIL Alnmouth and
Berwick
ROAD A1
Disabled parking

DUNSTANBURGH CASTLE 20
C/O 14 Queen Street
Alnwick NE66 1RD
TEL 01665 576231
OPEN 10-6 every day April-
end Sept and 10-5 Oct,
10-4 Wed-Sun Nov-March
Admission charge

EH members free
RAIL Alnmouth 8 miles
BUS Phone 01670 533128
ROAD 1.5 mile walk from
Craster

HEXHAM ABBEY 21
Hexham Northumberland
NE46 3NB
TEL 01434 602031
FAX 01434 606116
OPEN Oct-April 9-5
May-Sept 9-7pm
Tea room seats 50
OPEN June-Sept Tues
Sat and Sun 1-5
Disabled access partial
RAIL Hexham
BUS Newcastle-Carlisle
ROAD A69

WARKWORTH CASTLE 22
Warkworth
Northumberland
NE66 0UJ
TEL 01665711423
OPEN April-end Sept daily
10-6, Oct 10-5
Nov-March 10-4
Admission charge
EH members free
Disabled access: castle only
RAIL Alnmouth 3.5 miles
BUS Phone 01670 533128
ROAD A1068
Disabled parking

181

THE WIDLFOWL AND WETLANDS TRUST   23

District 15, Washington Tyne and Wear NE38 8LE
TEL *01914 165454*
FAX *01914 165801*
OPEN *every day except Christmas day*
Admission charge
WWT *members free*
Free access to tea room
Tea room seats 60
Disabled access
RAIL *Sunderland*
BUS *186 from Washington*
ROAD *A19 , A195, A 1231 & A182*
Disabled parking

WASHINGTON OLD HALL   23

The Avenue, Washington Village, NE38 7LE
TEL *01914 166879*
OPEN *April-Nov 11-5*
Phone in advance for other opening days
Admission charge
NT *members free*
Disabled access partial
RAIL *Heworth (metro)*
BUS *Phone 0191 2325325*
ROAD *A1*

BOLTON ABBEY ESTATE, PRIEST'S HOUSE   24

Barden Tower, Barden Skipton, North Yorks BD23 6AS
TEL *01756 720616*
FAX *01756 720330*
OPEN *Easter-end Oct Sat-Wed*
Ring for winter opening
Tea room seats 39
Disabled access: level but not easy
RAIL *Leeds to Ilkley*
ROAD *A59 then B16160*

BOLTON ABBEY ESTATE   25

Estate Office, Bolton Abbey, Skipton North Yorks BD23 6EX
TEL *01756 710533,*
FAX *01756 710535*
OPEN *Priory open every day 8.30-dusk*
Admission charge includes access to Priory Church and ruins, nature trails and moors

BOLTON ABBEY ESTATE, TEA COTTAGE   25

TEL *01756 710495*
Tea Cottage seats 90
OPEN *Easter-Oct every day weekends Oct-Easter*
Disabled access

RAIL *Ilkley via Leeds*
BUS *infrequent*
ROAD *A59 then B6100*
Disabled parking in village

BOROUGHBRIDGE TOURIST INFORMATION CENTRE   26

TEL *01423 323373*

NORTON CONYERS 26

Wath, Nr Ripon North Yorks
TEL *01765 640333*
OPEN *Bank Holiday Sun & Mon, most Sundays in June, July and August*
Teas served on Charity open days only
Admission charge
Disabled access
RAIL *Thirsk or Harrogate*
ROAD *A1*
Disabled parking

BOTTON VILLAGE   27

Danby, Whitby North Yorks YO21 2NJ
TEL *01287 66087*
Phone for admission details
RAIL *Danby or Castleton*
Disabled access

SEWERBY HALL AND GARDENS 28

*Church lane Sewerby
Bridlington East
Yorkshire YO15 1EA*
TEL *01262 677874*
OPEN *Apr-Oct 10-6, Winter
Sat-Tues (Phone for times)*
RAIL *Bridlington*
ROAD *A165*
BUS *pass Hall*

THE MUSEUM OF SOUTH YORKSHIRE LIFE 29

*Cusworth Hall,
Cusworth, Doncaster
South Yorks DN5 7TU*
TEL/FAX *01302 782342*
OPEN *Mon-Fri 10-5
Sat 11-5, Sun 1-5
Closes 4pm Dec-Jan
Free admission
Tea room seats 40
Disabled access on ground
floor*
RAIL *Doncaster*
BUS *42 and 189 from
Doncaster*
ROAD *A1(M) then A638
Disabled parking*

FOUNTAINS ABBEY AND STUDLEY ROYAL 30

*Studley Park, Ripon
North Yorks HG4 3DY*
TEL *01765 608888*
FAX *01765 608889*

OPEN *all year except Dec
24 and 25 and Fri in Nov,
Dec and Jan
Admission charge*
NT *members free
Tea room seats 200
Disabled access to tea room*
RAIL *Harrogate*
BUS *Limited bus service*
ROAD *B6265
Disabled parking
Minibus around estate*

HOWDEN MINSTER 31

East Yorkshire
OPEN *daily from 9-5
Ruins open at any
reasonable time*

PEN-Y-GHENT CAFE AND TOURIST INFORMATION CENTRE 32

*Horton-in-Ribblesdale
Settle, North Yorks
BD24 OHE*
TEL/FAX *01729 860333*
OPEN *9am-6pm daily
except Tuesday
Tea room seats 30
Disabled access to tea
room and centre
Parking at door*
RAIL *Horton-in-Ribblesdale*
ROAD *B6479*
BUS *3 per day except Sun*

PARCEVALL HALL GARDENS 33

*Skyreholme, Skipton
North Yorks BD23 6DE*
TEL *01756 720311*
OPEN *Good Friday - end
Oct every day 10-6
Admission charge
Tea room seats 20
Disabled access*
RAIL *Skipton*
BUS *from Skipton*
ROAD *B6265*

SHANDY HALL 34

*Coxwold, North Yorks
YO61 4AD*
TEL *01347 868465*
OPEN *beg June-end Sept
Wed 2-4.30, Sun 2.30-4.30
Gardens daily except Sat
beg May-end Sept
Admission charge
Partial disabled access*
ROAD *A19*

SKIPTON CASTLE 35

*Skipton North Yorks
BD23 1AQ*
TEL *01756 792442*
FAX *01756 796100*
OPEN *Daily March-Sept 10-6
Sun 12-6, Oct-Feb 10-4
Admission charge*
RAIL *Skipton*
BUS *many pass door*
ROAD *A59*

SKIPTON PARISH CHURCH   35
OPEN *daily*
Tea room opens Fri 10-4
Sat 10-4

THE CRAVEN MUSEUM SKIPTON   35
TEL *01756 706407*
OPEN *April-Sept daily*
except Tues (Phone for
admission details)

SLEDMERE HOUSE   36
Sledmere, Driffield
East Yorks
TEL *01377 236637*
FAX *01377 236500*
OPEN *Easter Fri-Tues, Bank*
Holidays, May-end Sept
closed Mon and Sat
Admission charge, free to
tea room
Tearoom seats 80
OPEN *Easter-end Sept*
Closed Mon
Disabled access to
tearoom
RAIL *Driffield*
BUS *137 from Driffield*
ROAD *B1253*
Disabled parking

MUKER VILLAGE STORES, TEA SHOP AND INFORMATION   37
Muker, Richmond
North Yorks DL11 6QG
TEL *01748 886409*

SWALEDALE FOLK MUSEUM   37
The Green, Reeth
Nr Richmond
North Yorks DL11 6QT
TEL *01748 884373*
OPEN *Good Friday to*
October 10.30-5, daily
Admission charge
RAIL *Nearest Darlington*
BUS *United bus 30*
ROAD *B26270*
Disabled access and
parking

THE NIDDERDALE MUSEUM   38
King Street, Pateley
Bridge, Harrogate, North
Yorks HG3 5LE
TEL *01423 711225*
OPEN *Easter-end Oct daily,*
winter Sat and Sun 2-5,
August school holidays
daily 11-5
Admission charge
Disabled stairlift
RAIL *Harrogate*
BUS *Harrogate to Pateley*
Bridge
ROAD *B6165 or B6265*
Disabled parking

LEYBURN TOURIST INFORMATION CENTRE   39
TEL *01969 623069*

WHARFEDALE CHURCHES   40
Call Diocesan Office for
more information on
opening times of these
churches
TEL *01274 725958*

CAPTAIN COOK MEMORIAL MUSEUM   41
Grape Lane, Whitby
North Yorkshire YO22 4BE
TEL/FAX *01947 601900*
OPEN *weekends March*
11-3, April-end Oct daily
9.45-5
Admission charge
RAIL *Whitby*
BUS *93 and 93A*
ROAD *A171*

WHITBY MUSEUM   41
Pannett park
Whitby
North Yorkshire YO21 1RE
TEL *01947 602908*
OPEN *Tues 10-1, Wed-Sat*
10-4, Sun 2-4
Amission charge

YORKSHIRE COUNTRY WINES 42

*Riverside Cellars, The Mill
Glasshouses near Pateley
Bridge, Harrogate
North Yorks HG3 5QH*
TEL *01423 711947*
FAX *01423 711223*
OPEN *Easter-end Oct Wed-
Sun 11.30-4.30, end Oct-
Easter Sat and Sun only
11.30-4.30
Winery tours Fri and Sat
Tea room seats 36 plus 16
outside
Restricted disabled access
Disabled parking 50yds*
RAIL *Harrogate*
BUS *Harrogate to Pateley
Bridge, Glasshouses stop*
ROAD *B6165*

FAIRFAX HOUSE 43

*Castlegate
York YO1 9RN*
TEL *01904 655543*
FAX *01904 652262*
OPEN *daily except Fri
Admission charge
Disabled access limited
Disabled parking 50 yds*

TREASURER'S HOUSE 44

*Minster Yard
York YO1 7JQ*
TEL *01904 624247*
FAX *01904 647372*
OPEN *end March-end Oct*

*daily, closed Fri
Admission charge*
NT *members free
Tea room seats 60,*
OPEN *as house
Free access to tea room
Ground floor accessible
with help to disabled,
steep stairs to tea room*
ROAD *Park and Ride
scheme, nearest car park
St John's off Lord Mayor's
Walk
Very limited disabled
parking by arrangement*

ST MARTIN'S LE GRAND 45

Coney St, York
OPEN *Sat, more frequent
opening planned*

THE SPURRIERGATE CENTRE 45

*St Michael's Church
Spurriergate
York YO1 1QR*
TEL *01904 629393*
FAX *01904 629383*
OPEN *10-4.30 Mon-Fri
9.30-5 Sat
Disabled access*

YORK TOURIST INFORMATION CENTRE 46

TEL *01904 621756*

ST WILLIAM'S RESTAURANT 47

*College street
York YO1 2JF*
OPEN *every day 10-5
Every evening 6-9.30
Restaurant seats 80.
Disabled access limited*

YORK CITY ART GALLERY 47

*Exhibition Square
York YO1 7EW*
TEL *01904 551861*
FAX *01904 551866*
OPEN *Monday to Sat 10-5
Sun 2.30-5. Closed Jan 1,
Good Fri and Dec 25-26
Disabled access
Disabled parking: drop off
at main door*

THE MERCHANT ADVENTURERS 47

Fossgate, York YO1 9XD
TEL/FAX *01904 654818*
OPEN *March-November 9-5
Winter 9-3
Partial disabled access
Admission charge*

YORK MINSTER 47

*Dean gate, York YO17HH
(visitors department)*
TEL *01904 639347*
FAX *01904 613049*
OPEN *every day
Admission free
Donations accepted*

Index

Photographs by the author except page 87 with the kind permission of the Trustees of The Chatsworth Settlement.

Author's photograph by Richard Easton

Front cover illustrations Don Pottery Pattern Book 1807 with permission of the Doncaster Museum Service, Doncaster Metropolitan Borough Council.